Sexual Healing

❤

Barbara Keesling, Ph.D., holds a doctorate in
in health and social psychology from the
University of California. She has been a
surrogate partner since 1980 and consults
with many sex therapists.

Her familiarity with relevant psychological
theory and research and her experiences
treating clients make her uniquely qualified to
write a book describing the treatment
techniques that have recently emerged from
the profession of surrogate partner therapy.

Dr. Keesling lives in Southern California. She
is currently visiting Assistant Professor of
Psychology at the University of California,
Riverside.

This book is dedicated to my clients

Sexual Healing

❤

A Self-Help Program
to Enhance Your Sensuality
and Overcome
Common Sexual Problems

Barbara Keesling, Ph.D.

© Barbara Keesling, 1990

First U.S. edition published in 1990 by Hunter House Inc., Publishers

Library of Congress Cataloging-in-Publication Data:

Keesling, Barbara.
    Sexual healing : a self-help program to enhance your
sensuality and overcome common sexual problems / by Barbara
Keesling. — 1st U.S. ed.
      p. cm.
    Includes bibliographical references.
    Includes index.
    ISBN 0-89793-066-5 : $22.95. — ISBN 0-89793-067-3 (pbk.) : $12.95
    1. Sex instruction. 2. Sex (Psychology) I. Title.
HQ31.K39 1990
613.9'6—dc20   89-26726

Book and cover design by Qalagraphia
Cover calligraphy by Luis R. Caughman
Copy editing by Jackie Melvin and Stephanie Hoppe
Production manager: Paul J. Frindt
Set in Cheltenham by 847 Communications, Claremont, CA
Printed by Delta Lithograph Co., Valencia, CA
Manufactured in the United States of America

10 9 8 7 6 5 4 3 2 1

Table of Contents

❤

Acknowledgments

❤

I would like to thank all of the people who helped with this book.

Many of the exercises described in *Sexual Healing* were taught to me by Ron Gibb, Anita Banker, Michael Riskin, and James Gibbons. They learned many of the sensate focus exercises from Barbara Roberts, a Los Angeles therapist.

I would like to thank my publisher, Kiran Rana, and my editors, Jackie Melvin and Stephanie Hoppe, as well as the staff at Hunter House.

Bob Cialdini was extremely helpful in giving me feedback on the book in its early stages.

I would also like to thank my husband, Al, for encouraging me to write a book about my experiences, and for encouraging me to go to graduate school.

An Introduction to Sexual Healing

❤

There are two kinds of books written to help people with their sex life. One kind, usually written by doctors and sex therapists, describes the sex therapy that is used to help people to overcome common sexual problems, such as erection or ejaculation problems in men and inhibited arousal or inhibited orgasm in women. The other kind, usually written by sexologists or sex experts, describes techniques and approaches that can be used to develop new sexual attitudes and enhance sexual pleasure.

This book is unique because its approach includes both people who are functional but wish to improve their sexual experiences and those who may have specific problems. This is sexual healing in the broadest sense: a program that can help anyone, at any level, from physical sexual functioning to deep personal and emotional experience. As you become sexually healthy and more sensually aware, your sexual activities can become so relaxing and enjoyable that your sexual expression can have a healing effect on your mind, your body, and your relationships.

❤

I have been a professional sexual surrogate partner for nine years, and I am a doctor of psychology. As a surrogate partner, I have done both *sensual* and *sexual* exercises with men who had been experiencing common sexual dysfunctions, such as erection problems or premature ejaculation. As a social psychologist, I have studied how the presence of others can influence our thoughts, feelings, and behavior, and how these concepts can be used to structure positive sexual interactions. This book is written from the understanding I have acquired of these two aspects of sexual healing.

I began to work as a surrogate partner in 1980, after reading a newspaper account about surrogate partners and what they do. The article interested me and inspired me to seek training. At that time, I had just started college and was majoring in psychology. I continued to work as a surrogate partner to support myself through a Master's degree in Experimental Psychology and a doctorate in Health and Social Psychology.

About two years into my Ph.D. program, I noticed that I was enjoying my surrogate work more and my clients were progressing through therapy more quickly, learning the sensual and sexual exercises with fewer problems. What had changed? Was I getting smarter, or was what I was learning in college having a specific effect on my work?

Some of the important topics that social psychologists study include nonverbal communication, interpersonal attraction, how we share our feelings and thoughts with others, and how we put psychological pressure on others and respond to pressure from them. When I unconsciously started using this information in my work, I became a better surrogate partner because I intuitively learned not to put pressure on myself or my partners.

It gradually became clear to me that many authors of sexual self-help books do not recognize the importance of these issues. I have probably read every sex manual that has been written in the past thirty years, because I am always in search of material I can use to help my clients. I found, however, that these books rarely contained any information that I could use. Why, when so many books purported to describe the secrets of "good sex" or even "great sex," was this material so uninspiring? I concluded that I uncovered so little of value because the work that my surrogate partner colleagues and I do with clients has advanced beyond the techniques known to these authors.

The field of sex therapy has come a long way in the past thirty years. People with sexual problems such as an inability to have an orgasm or an erection can now be helped. I believe *Sexual Healing* will advance the current status of sex therapy by describing in detail exercises that you can safely use at home, exercises that sex therapists *today* recommend for their clients.

In the sections below, I discuss some of the important ways in which *Sexual Healing* differs from other books on sexuality.

Defining the Audience

Often, authors of sexual self-help books do not specify for which audience a particular book is intended, or they imply that the book is "for everyone," when in fact it is not. There are a number of audiences to whom books on sexuality may be directed: 1) people who are sexually functional but want to put some excitement into their sex lives; 2) people who are experiencing specific sexual problems; 3) people who are interested in learning facts about sexual behavior; and 4) professionals, such as medical doctors and therapists.

Confusion may develop when people who are experiencing sexual problems read books which are really intended for professional audiences and attempt to apply the information and ideas at home. Frustration can also occur when people who are experiencing sexual problems or have little sexual experience read books intended for fully functional, experienced readers who are looking for some added zest.

If this has happened to you, you may have blamed yourself for failing to benefit from reading those books. It is not your fault if you did not gain anything—it takes more than a change of attitude or knowledge of sexual facts to change ingrained sexual habits.

Learning New Sexual Behaviors

Books that promote positive attitudes toward sexuality often fail to provide basic, detailed instructions for improving your sex life or for preventing sexual problems. Books such as these may have left you with the impression that all it takes to improve your sex life is a positive attitude, which is definitely not the case—gradual changes in specific sexual activities are also necessary.

In *Sexual Healing*, you will learn these specific activities. These sensual and sexual exercises can be done *before* your attitudes change about sex. Doing these relaxing sensual and sexual activities will help you develop more positive attitudes toward your sexuality.

Self-help books which *do* provide more specific instructions about sexual activities often promote practices that can lead to increased feelings of pressure to perform rather than giving you permission to enjoy yourself. These practices often instruct you to try to please your partner.

In *Sexual Healing*, you will learn to focus on your own pleasure and enjoyment. Learning about your *own* natural sexual response will actually make you better able to appreciate and enjoy your partner's response. You will start at a basic level in learning new sexual behaviors and attitudes. The ideas of pleasing *yourself*, knowing your *own* body, and learning about *your* natural sexual response are so important that I have emphasized them throughout this book. Learning to trust yourself and your own feelings will be a continuing theme throughout *Sexual Healing.*

Learning to Reduce Anxiety

Most sexual self-help books cite anxiety as the most damaging immediate cause of sexual problems. Yet their authors frequently encourage readers to perform activities which lead to more rather than less anxiety (such as focusing on your partner's response rather than your own response).

Anxiety in a sexual situation is a combination of physical responses, such as rapid breathing, and mental concerns, such as, "What will happen next?" People become anxious in sexual encounters because they perceive that their partner expects them to have an erection, have an orgasm, be able to delay ejaculation, etc.

The way to remove performance anxiety is to learn to concentrate on your own feelings of enjoyment and sexual arousal. In *Sexual Healing,* you will learn how to focus on your feelings in order to reduce performance anxiety. You will also learn how to avoid putting performance pressure on your partner, so that both of you can fully enjoy your sexual encounters. You will learn specific techniques for recognizing and reducing your own anxiety in sexual situations, so that you will no longer engage in sexual activities that increase anxiety.

The authors of many sexual self-help books describe ways to create "moods" for sex, implying that you will not be able to have satisfactory or enjoyable sex unless you are already in a sexy or aroused mood. The only preparation you must make in order to experience sexual healing is to be in a neutral or receptive mood. Emphasis in other books has been on setting the scene for sex or making oneself attractive for the partner. Here you will

learn to enjoy sex more by focusing on your own pleasure and sexual needs rather than on worries about your
partner's likes and dislikes.

People who are experiencing sexual problems often
think that they need to *add* something in order to improve their sexual activities. In fact, if you are experiencing sexual problems, you probably need to *subtract*
something from your sexual encounters—anxiety or the
stress that has built up over the day or week.

Sexual healing does not rely on the addition of
candlelight, bubble baths, perfume, X-rated videotapes,
or exotic lingerie. If you are one of the millions of people
who feel a stomach-churning anxiety or even mild discomfort before or during sexual activity, or if you enjoy
sex but often find yourself thinking about something else
during sexual activities, the use of mood-setters or props
will not help you. (They may even make you feel even
more anxious due to increased pressure to perform.)
And if you are sexually functional, these props will not
improve your sex life if your *partner* is experiencing
anxiety.

In *Sexual Healing,* you will learn to reach a receptive
or neutral mood state in order to enjoy sexuality, rather
than expect yourself to feel sexually aroused before you
allow yourself to experience any sexual stimulation. You
will learn to do activities in order to relieve stress and
feel sexually aroused, rather than expect yourself to
spontaneously generate sexual feelings.

Focusing on Your Feelings

Many books designed to help you improve your sex life
rely on the teaching of single techniques, such as the
squeeze technique for premature ejaculation, in which
the woman squeezes the tip of the man's penis when he
feels ready to ejaculate. Techniques such as squeezing
the penis or tugging on the testicles rely on external

intervention by the partner, and promote a mechanical rather than a sensual attitude toward the body. In addition, in my practice as a surrogate partner, I have noted that many clients find these techniques aversive and that the use of them tends to cause more problems. Also, they are somewhat difficult to do.

In *Sexual Healing,* you will learn to focus on your own feelings and sensations of arousal in order to maximize your natural responses, rather than rely on the application of external treatments. You will learn a full, step-by-step program of techniques that are fun, feel good, and are easy to use.

Books on sexuality which *do* provide information on focusing on your arousal do not generally provide enough information so that you can use the techniques successfully. This may be because the authors do not really understand these techniques and the reasons for using them, or have not done the activities themselves. The reason *Sexual Healing* differs from other books that are available is that I have worked with clients at the skin-to-skin level. I know what activities promote sexual functioning and enjoyment because I have helped hundreds of clients through the sexual healing process.

Sensuality and Eroticism

Sexual Healing does make use of material from other sex therapists and authors. For example, you will learn how to do "sensate focus," a valuable and established technique for increasing relaxation, sensual arousal, and sexual arousal.

The most important thing you will learn in *Sexual Healing* is how to interact with your partner in a sensuous way. *Sensuality is the enjoyment and appreciation of how your body feels, especially when it is touching or being touched.* Touching another person, being touched by another person, feeling rain on your face, petting an animal—these can all be sensual or sensuous experiences.

Sensuality, as described in this book, should be distinguished from eroticism. Erotic materials are designed to excite you sexually, usually through your sense of vision, or through reading and fantasy. People who create erotic materials do so with the idea that others will become sexually aroused from viewing or reading these materials.

Both sensuality and eroticism have a place in your life and in your expression of your sexuality. But reliance on eroticism to the exclusion of sensuality can actually *cause* sexual problems. We live in a society that places a high value on eroticism, but a very low value on sensuality. Sensuality is in a sense more basic, as it is pure gratification of the body, with little or no mental component involved. The exercises in this book will teach you to return to a state of basic enjoyment of your body, without which full appreciation of eroticism is probably not possible.

Many of the exercises described in this book will no doubt sexually stimulate you. However, the initial reason for doing the exercises is to learn sensuality—how your skin feels. If developing your ability to focus on sensual enjoyment becomes your main purpose in doing the activities described here, you have a good chance of normalizing your sexual functioning, and also reaching a state of heightened sexual arousal and intimacy with your partner.

What You Will Not Learn

There are also several things you will *not* learn in this book. You will not learn to become a great lover or to impress your partners with your sexual prowess. You will not learn to be "incredible in bed" or to "give great head." Instead, you will learn to enjoy your sexuality and do what feels good for you. You will learn how to enjoy sexual activities rather than how to "perform" them.

This book will probably not provide titillating night-table reading. (It doesn't even have pictures!) Reading through the exercises in this book or looking at pictures will not help enhance your sensuality. Experiencing the exercises will.

You should also abandon any ideas of using this book by yourself and "surprising" your spouse or partner with the results. For this program to promote your enjoyment, it is necessary for both members of the couple to be equally familiar with the exercises. Wanting to surprise your partner with newfound sexual prowess is an attitude which could interfere with the process described in this book, as it reinforces the idea of sex as performance. If you do not have a sexual partner with whom to practice these exercises, exercises are provided for you to practice alone. But some of the advanced exercises yield their full benefits only if you do them with a partner.

Who Can Use This Book

Many of us feel we have problems with some area of our sexuality. These are not usually problems in a clinical sense, but they represent areas of vulnerability which we may have long wanted to explore more deeply and to heal. The approach and exercises described in *Sexual Healing* provide a perfect foundation for doing this. Readers will learn to start over sexually, ridding themselves of bad habits and preventing future sexual problems. You will develop the power to use your sexual activities as healing experiences for you and your partner, rather than experiencing sex as disappointing, frustrating, or boring.

People who are experiencing common problems in sexual functioning will also be able to help themselves, in the privacy of their homes, with trusted partners. For men, some of these problems are ejaculating too soon (rapid ejaculation), not being able to ejaculate at all (inhibited ejaculation), and not being able to have or keep an erection. For women, these problems include not being able to have an orgasm and inability to have intercourse because of closing up of the vaginal muscles (vaginismus). Members of both sexes may experience a fear of sex (sexual phobia) or a lack of sexual desire. These problems are discussed in detail in the book.

The exercises in the book will be most beneficial for people whose sexual problems are of short duration; in other words, when problems have been occurring for less than two years or so. In cases where the problems have been continuing for five, ten, or even twenty or more years, it is better to contact a qualified sex therapist rather than to rely on self-help. If you have had a severe sexual problem for quite a number of years, the exercises cannot hurt you and are unlikely to make your problem worse, but they should be done under the guidance of a therapist.

Sexual Healing will also be helpful to people who have little or no sexual experience. The exercises described here provide nonthreatening, relaxing, and gradual ways to initiate healthy sexual contact.

The book will also be of help to people who have significant medical problems or injuries that have affected their sexuality. These exercises can provide a way for you and your partner to comfortably explore your sexuality in a nonthreatening atmosphere. (The exercises in this book are not strenuous, but if you have a history of medical problems you should consult your physician before beginning the program.)

Finally, therapists will be able to use this book as a basis for helping sexually dysfunctional clients, as the exercises and the rationale behind them are described in detail.

The exercises in this book will work best for committed couples, whether one or both have sexual problems. However, if as a couple you have mutual sexual problems of long duration, you are probably experiencing communication and relationship problems which are unlikely to be helped by treating only the sexual issues. Here again, the assistance of a qualified sex therapist is recommended. In that case, you may wish to read this book to familiarize yourself with typical exercises which are part of a sex therapy program.

Although the case histories I include are drawn from heterosexual clients and exercises are often described as being done by opposite-sex partners, these exercises can also be done by same-sex partners with appropriate adjustments.

The Organization of This Book

Part I starts with a close look at healthy sexuality and the relationship between sensuality and touch. It explains the importance of sensuality, especially of learning how to focus on sensations in the here and now. This is followed by a review of common sexual problems.

In **Part II** you will first learn sensual and sexual exercises to do by yourself. There is a detailed discussion of how to relieve sexual anxiety, followed by the basic couple exercises in the sensate focus program. These basic exercises will provide you with a foundation for the more advanced exercises.

Part III contains advanced exercises for specific sexual concerns. I also show you how to tailor your program to your particular needs and interests and discuss what lies beyond the program, the realms of mutuality and intimacy.

Finally, **Appendix I** repeats the main points to remember when doing any sensate focus exercise (found at the end of Chapter 5), which I call "The Sensual

Mindset." It also includes general Guidelines for Feedback, which will help you remember what to discuss in the feedback session that follows every exercise. **Appendix II** lists all of the exercises in the book with their page references. **Appendix III** answers, for those who are interested, the questions I am most often asked about what surrogate partners do.

❤

Whether you are reading *Sexual Healing* to enhance your sexuality or in order to deal with a specific sexual problem, I hope you will learn, above all, the importance of sensuality. Enjoy yourself.

Part I

❤

Healthy Sexuality

Chapter 1

❤

Sexuality: Body and Mind

One of the areas in which I received my Ph.D. is called health psychology. Health psychology is a relatively new area of psychology, and health psychologists study the ways in which our body (our physical self) and our mind (our psychological self) interact and affect each other. This chapter will give you some information about physical and psychological aspects of sexuality which will help you understand your body's natural sexual response.

Historically, psychologists have focused their study on the mind rather than the body. Recent advances in both psychology and medicine have shown the importance of considering the body and the mind as a single unit, a whole. The mind and the body function together, but they interact in a way that makes them *seem* separate to us. In other words, it is possible for us to be more aware of one or the other at a given time.

What is the importance of this for our sexuality?

Sexuality and sexual activity are areas in which the mind and the body interact closely. Whether we experience sexual issues as mental or physical, research shows that we need to work with *both* the body and the mind to enhance our sexual awareness and resolve sexual problems.

A basic concept in health psychology is the idea that all physical problems have psychological aspects, and many (if not all) psychological problems have physical aspects. This idea is the foundation for the program described in this book. At times we will focus more on the body, and at other times we will turn our attention to the mind, but the end result will be that you will learn to experience both the physical and mental aspects of sexual arousal and enjoyment.

How Our Bodies Work: Sexual Response

There are several aspects of *physical* sexual functioning that you should know about before you do the activities described in this book.

The sex therapists Masters and Johnson described the sexual response cycle, which progresses from excitement to plateau to orgasm to resolution. They described these phases of the sexual response cycle in terms of physiological changes; for example, the excitement phase includes erection in the man and vaginal lubrication in the woman. Problems may arise at any phase of the response cycle. (For example, premature ejaculation is a problem of the orgasm phase.) Trying to recognize these physical phases in order to deal with sexual problems has frustrated many people.

In this book we are going to use a different system, not the physical sexual response cycle, for describing your sexual experiences, a simple scale for how aroused you *feel*, rather than how your body is responding. In other words, we will use a psychological scale for describing sexual arousal instead of a scale based on what changes are occurring in your body. Learning to become aware of your psychological level of arousal will help you become more aware of your physical arousal.

Your body obviously *does* go through changes during sexual activity. However, there are often misconceptions about these body responses. For example, many men assume that ejaculation and orgasm are the same thing, which they are not. Ejaculation is the expulsion of semen. Orgasm is the combination of rhythmic pelvic muscle contractions and a psychological sense of release. Ejaculation can occur with or without psychological arousal, because it is a reflex. It can also occur without erection. Both orgasm and ejaculation can occur with psychological stimulation only. Sexual problems can occur for men when orgasms happen without erections, or when arousal is not followed by orgasm.

Our psychological or mental sense of arousal and our physical sexual response usually run parallel to each other. Problems occur when there is some discrepancy between these two aspects. The exercises in this book can help to bring the physical and psychological parts of your sexual response back together if they have become separated.

How Our Bodies Work: Anxiety and Relaxation

In addition to the idea that both mind and body changes are involved in sexuality, there is an aspect of physiology with which you need to be familiar. This is the fact that there are two separate and contradictory sub-systems within our nervous system. One of these (the sympathetic nervous system) is responsible for speeding up our physical responses. If this system is active you will experience a combination of physical signs, such as rapid heartbeat and perspiration, and psychological signs, such as a feeling of *anxiety*. This is the system that delivers the so-called fight or flight response. Your body energy is mobilized so that you can fight, run away, or otherwise deal with a threatening event.

The other sub-system (the parasympathetic nervous system) is active when your body is taking care of its life-sustaining processes, like digestion. It is responsible for slowing your body down so that you can conserve energy; we experience the activity of this system as *relaxation*.

These two nervous systems are not active at the same time. You cannot be relaxed when you are anxious or aroused. Another way of saying this is that anxiety and relaxation are "incompatible responses."

Many sexual problems are caused by anxiety—the sympathetic nervous system working when it should not. People learn to react to a sexual situation with the fight or flight anxiety response. This anxiety then prevents them from becoming sexually aroused. If your sympathetic nervous system is engaged so that you are anxious, you will be unable to properly experience even the earliest phase of the sexual response cycle.

Because of how these two nervous systems function, it is impossible to turn off the sympathetic nervous system by *trying* to turn it off. If you *try* to turn it off, you will become *more* rather than less anxious. The only way to turn off the anxiety is to turn *on* the parasympathetic or relaxation system. The exercises in this book will show you how to do that by using specific relaxation techniques.

Sexuality and Mental Health

The sexual drive is different from other basic biological drives, such as hunger and thirst, in that a person can live without participating in sexual acts or reproducing. Even though research on sexuality and its effect on mental health is very sparse, we know that there are a number of ways in which positive sexual activity can contribute to our mental health. Our sexual feelings and expressions are a significant source of personal fulfillment and thus can enhance our mental well-being. Sexual expression may also contribute to our mental health in an indirect way. For example, sexual contact may provide a buffer against stress. The process of physical touching or nonsexual contact has been found to have a number of psychological benefits.

Positive sexual activity (which is any sexual activity that is viewed in a positive light by the person who experiences it) is one form of what psychologists call "social support." Social support refers to the human contact that people have available to them or imagine that they have available to them. I think of it as having other people available to provide positive emotional experiences. Research shows that the quality of social support is related to physical and mental health, with higher levels of social support being related to better health. Satisfying sexual contact can be one form of positive social support. In addition, one of the most important types of social support is having a person with whom to "self-disclose," a person with whom one may express feelings openly and talk about them. A satisfying sexual relationship provides an excellent atmosphere in which to share feelings, and this sharing of feelings has been found by psychologists to be linked to mental and physical health.

Our Bodies Affect Our Minds

The study of how changes in the body affect the mind is called "somatopsychology." This is the idea that physically moving the body into certain positions or performing certain physical activities can influence our psychological states, particularly our moods.

Here are some examples. If we move our facial

muscles into expressions of emotions, we will experience the emotions to some degree. In psychology laboratories, people who are instructed to turn the corners of their mouths up and hold them that way report more feelings of happiness than people who are not asked to move their faces. In fact, one way by which many women have been taught to have orgasms is to imitate the facial expressions and body position changes of orgasm. (You will learn this technique in a later chapter—despite the name, this is not the same as "faking" an orgasm for your partner's satisfaction).

Another example of how body changes can cause mental changes is the consistent finding that physical exercise (for example, jogging, aerobics, or cycling) decreases depression and anxiety and increases positive emotional states. Physical exercise stimulates the production of endorphins, which are brain chemicals that act as natural painkillers. *States of sexual arousal have also been found to produce these natural painkillers.* Thus the cliché, "Not tonight; I have a headache," may be contradictory, because sexual activity might be a natural way to relieve pain. In fact, sexual activity has recently been found to relieve symptoms of migraine headaches.

The field of bioenergetic psychotherapy also supports the idea that the body influences the mind. Bioenergetics, as described by Alexander Lowen (based on the psychological theories of Wilhelm Reich), is a type of therapy that uses the idea that our psychological conflicts are expressed in the ways in which we hold our bodies. By helping clients change their body positions, bioenergetic therapists hope to help them understand and resolve these conflicts.

Another important way that we can change our minds by changing our bodies is through touching and allowing ourselves to be touched. *Sexuality provides a context in which we can experience this healing touch.* For many of us, and especially for men, sexual encounters are often the only situations in which we are allowed to touch other human beings or to enjoy being touched by them. We may have been touched as children, but social norms for adults in North American culture do not provide for much physical contact.

Touching has been a traditional treatment for illness throughout human history. Touch may communicate a number of things, such as relaxation, comfort, and non-verbal expectations. In fact, there is quite a bit of research on the positive effects of touch. Since a major focus of this book is on learning nonsexual touching, I would like to share some of this evidence with you.

Much of the research on touch and health has been brought together by Ashley Montagu in his classic book *Touching*. Montagu describes the effect of skin contact on mental and physical health throughout all stages of the lifespan, beginning with the birth experience.

His book shows that touch is vitally important for humans of all ages, as well as for other animals. Infant monkeys who are deprived of touch have problems with their sexual behavior in later life. Human infants who are deprived of contact have higher death rates than those who are touched. In human adults, being touched has been shown to lower heart rate and blood pressure and promote physical relaxation in general. Research shows that even stroking a pet can lower one's blood pressure and heart rate. Touching may also have a positive effect on the immune system. Montagu describes research on rats which shows that rats who are handled when they are young have better developed immune systems as adults.

So it is clear that touch is necessary for infants to develop properly. Although there is no research on whether adults *need* touch, there is also no reason to believe that our need to be touched ends with childhood. The desire to be held or touched may be a major motive for engaging in sexual activities.

Touching also makes it easier to share feelings. It has been noted that patients who are touched in the genital region by doctors and nurses during the course of a physical examination often confide personal sexual information. It seems that being touched in intimate areas brings intimate thoughts and feelings to the surface.

Being touched has been shown to have positive effects on adults in medical settings. For example, in one study, patients who were touched by nurses recovered faster than those who were not touched. It is not known precisely *how* touching in this situation helps people get better. It could be that the touch directly promotes relaxation through the activation of the parasympathetic nervous system. Or it could be that the act of touching communicates the expectation that the patient will get well.

All of this is evidence for the idea that changing our bodies will change our minds. The sexual exercises, touching, and body movements you will learn from this book will directly affect your emotional state. Rather than needing to "get in the mood" before you experience sexual activities, you will learn to do body activities that will decrease depression and anxiety and promote positive mood states such as feelings of relaxation.

Our Minds Affect Our Bodies

Most people are familiar with the concept of psychosomatic illness—the idea that our mental states, such as attitudes and emotions, can influence whether we get sick or not, how quickly we get better, or even the development of chronic health problems such as heart disease and cancer. The idea that an illness is psychosomatic does not mean that it is "all in one's head" or is not real. It means that our psychology plays some part in it, no matter how small. In a sense, all medical problems are psychosomatic, because being sick affects us psychologically. The fact that the mind can influence the body has made it possible to design treatments for cancer that include aspects such as relaxation and visualization.

What is the tie-in to sexuality? People experiencing sexual problems often report one or more psychosomatic symptoms such as migraine headaches, stomach problems, or skin problems. When their sexual problem is successfully treated, their medical problems often become less severe or disappear entirely.

Sigmund Freud was the first to examine psychosomatic illness and its tie-in to sexuality. Freud thought that repressed sexual conflicts could emerge as physical symptoms, and he seems to have been right. If sexual interactions are a source of conflict or anxiety for you, this could definitely have a negative effect on your physical health. Many people intuitively recognize that their sexual interactions are a source of stress and attempt to avoid sexual activity. Unfortunately, denying the problem will not make it go away, and many people find that even if they give up sexual activities, their psychosomatic complaints remain. The complaints may take on a different physical form, but they remain because the lack of sexual activity is still a source of unconscious conflict.

If you have a fear of sexuality that is reflected in health problems, the exercises in this book provide a way to relearn your sexual expression in a gradual and nonthreatening manner, and to use this positive sexual experience as a way to heal your body and your mind.

Let me caution you that the relationship between sexuality and health has not been *proven* by psychologists—we only know that these things seem to be related to each other in predictable ways. I would like to be able to say that improving your sex life will improve your overall physical and mental health. However, there is no absolute scientific proof that positive sexual activity keeps you healthy or that lack of sexual expression causes illness. Believe it or not, no psychologist has ever tried to research this question!

Based on my experience with clients, it does appear that many people who are cured of sexual problems find that certain health problems they had been experiencing go away. And it is definitely the case that resolving a sexual problem results in lower levels of anxiety and depression, which can in turn reduce health problems.

What is Healthy Sexuality?

How do you know when—or if—your sexuality has become a problem?

Healthy sexuality does not mean flawless functioning. For example, it is completely normal for a man to ejaculate quickly once in a while. It is completely normal for a man to *want* to ejaculate quickly once in a while. It is normal for a man to not be able to have an erection or an ejaculation once in a while. It is completely normal for a woman to not be able to have an orgasm once in a while, and it is perfectly normal for a woman to not *want* to have an orgasm once in a while. It is very normal to have a temporarily low desire for sexual activity. It is very normal to experience some instances of sexual activity as being more satisfying than others. None of these conditions means that there is something wrong with you.

Healthy sexuality is not defined by the types of activities you do or how often you do them. Most of us seem to have a desire to compare ourselves with other people, to find out whether we are having the same types of sexual activities as other people are having, or whether we are having sexual activities as often as they are. If you spend too much energy comparing yourself with other people sexually, you will develop a performance-oriented attitude that will interfere with the arousal and intimacy you could be experiencing.

Everyone has a different level of desire for sexual activity. That is why in *Sexual Healing* we will define healthy sexuality in terms of your feelings about yourself. You have a sexual problem if your sexuality is causing you personal distress, such as anxiety, depression, or fear. If you feel that you have a sexual problem, then you probably do have one, because any amount of worrying about sex will interfere with your body's ability to function.

The exercises in this book will benefit you most if you begin them with a healthy attitude. A healthy attitude is, "I want to enjoy myself and increase my sexual arousal." Not-so-healthy attitudes are, "I want to work at getting better," or, "I want to last longer than everybody else," or, "I want to have an erection or an orgasm even when I don't feel like it."

It is tempting to want to think of the body as a machine that is not performing the way we want it to. The fact that we have a mind that can influence our body and be influenced by it makes it unproductive to think of the body in this mechanical way.

❤

Because our mind and body interact so closely, *sexuality is full of paradoxes*. For example:

- The harder you try to make something happen sexually, the less will happen.

- The way to cure your sexual problem is to not try to cure it.

- The way to be able to have sexual activity when-ever you want to is to learn to recognize when you do not want to have sexual activity.

- The way to learn to relax is to learn to recognize when you are anxious.

- The way to learn to concentrate is to recognize when you are not concentrating.

- The way to be able to please your partner is to learn what feels good for *you*.

Perhaps the biggest paradox is that, while doing the exercises you will learn in this program, you may feel that you are not "working on your problem" at all! I am not trying to speak in riddles or confuse you. I am trying to offer you a new perspective, which focuses on a different way of thinking about sensual and sexual activity. The exercises *will* produce changes in your body and mind, even if you do not recognize those changes immediately.

Chapter 2

❤

Sensuality and Touch

In the last chapter we talked about the importance of touch. We are now ready to go into more detail about the exercises which I consider to be the core of the book. These are called "sensate focus" exercises and originated in the work of the sex therapists Masters and Johnson.

The name "sensate focus" may sound quite technical but is actually self-explanatory: Throughout the exercises you are to *focus* your attention as closely as you can on your *sensations*. This is the essence of the exercises. Always focus all your attention on your skin where it comes in contact with your partner's skin. If your mind wanders off during the exercise, bring it back to the exact point of contact between your skin and your partner's skin.

This way of touching has been proven to remove the pressure to perform, to allow each person to touch for his or her own pleasure, and to facilitate the communication of tenderness, caring, and gentleness. I will call this touch a caress.

Other books may refer to this kind of touch as "sensual massage" but, strictly speaking, it is not. A massage is generally a manipulation of the large muscles of the body performed for the benefit of the person being massaged. If you have done sensual massage with sexual partners before and felt some anxiety, it is probably because the occasion became a performance situation. Chances are that you felt that your partner expected you to do a good job, or you worried what your partner was thinking about the job you were doing. Sensate focus exercises are designed to relieve this kind of anxiety, because they are done for your *own* pleasure.

The Touch

There are no specific caress techniques. Caress in the way that feels best for you, within these guidelines: Your caress should be light and very, very slow. Remember that *touching and being touched in a slow, sensuous, or comforting way relaxes us.* A rapid or heavy touch triggers the sympathetic rather than the parasympathetic nervous system and conveys a sense of psychological pressure that is not relaxing for either person.

I find that the best position for any caress is one which enables touching with the least physical exertion. For example, for a back caress, rather than straddling your partner, try lying in full body contact with your partner while you touch your partner's back with one hand. Touch for your own pleasure and explore whatever part of your partner's back feels good to you. If you feel very relaxed, you may want to expand the caress to use not only the palm of your hand but also the back of your hand or even your face or hair.

Always maintain contact with your partner. Avoid surprising your partner with a sudden touch when you switch hands. If you use lotion or body oil for a caress (use it only if *you* want to, not simply because your partner wants you to), warm the lotion or oil in your hand before you apply it, and maintain contact with your partner's body when you re-apply lotion.

Explore your partner's body for your own pleasure. You may use either long, sweeping strokes or short ones. This is up to you. Try them both and use the one that feels good for you.

I cannot emphasize slowness enough! If you think that you are moving your hand slowly enough, consciously cut your speed in half and see how this affects your ability to focus on the touch. Do not worry about whether your partner is enjoying the caress. It will be his or her responsibility to let you know whether you are doing something that is uncomfortable. Sensate focus exercises are intended to promote relaxation. Both you and your partner will feel more free to relax if the exercises are done very slowly, with eyes closed and without talking. *You cannot caress too slowly.*

To begin with, you may feel that you are focusing on the sensations in your skin only part of the time—perhaps half the time or even less. It is normal to become distracted now and then. Simply recognize that your mind is suddenly elsewhere and bring it back to the place where your skin makes contact with your partner's skin. Repeat each exercise until you focus on sensations most of the time.

Active and Passive Roles

Most sensate focus exercises for couples start with one person as the active partner and the other as passive, then the partners switch roles.

When you are the active partner, do the caress as instructed and try to keep your attention on exactly where your skin touches your partner's skin. Do not speak to your partner during the exercise or ask for any feedback. Assume that the caress feels good or at least neutral to your partner. When you have finished, tell your partner you are done.

When you are the passive partner, lie in a relaxed position. Relax any muscles that feel tense. Pay attention to exactly where your partner touches your skin. Mentally follow your partner's hand as it caresses your body. Do not respond to your partner in any way. Do not tell him or her what to do or moan and wriggle around or make any other sign. The only time you should give your partner any feedback is if he or she does something that hurts you or makes you feel uncomfortable (for example, rubbing too hard or scraping a nipple by accident). Remaining passive will allow your body to experience your sensual arousal fully.

As you read the instructions for the active and passive roles for each exercise, you may be concerned that this is not the way in which sexual encounters proceed in real life. In real-life sexual encounters, both partners do various activities, often simultaneously.

But in real-life sexual encounters partners often intentionally or unintentionally pressure each other to perform sexually, and in real-life sexual encounters partners often worry about what the other person is thinking or what the other person would like. People spend a lot of time in real-life sexual encounters being distracted.

The program I describe here is innovative. It teaches you to free yourself of intrusive thoughts like, "I wonder if she's really enjoying this." By concentrating totally on where your skin touches your partner's skin, you will be *fully involved and present in what you are doing*. And although only one person is active at a time, there is an aspect of mutuality, because both partners are focusing on the same thing at the same time. You will find this is actually more sensually arousing than when you and your partner are doing different activities at the same time.

The reason for artificially breaking down the sexual encounter into clearly defined active and passive roles at this stage is very simple: You need to experience *non-demand interaction*. You avoid giving feedback to your partner while you take the passive role so that your partner can touch for his or her own pleasure without having to worry about what you like or want. Similarly, when you are in the active role, you should touch for your own pleasure without worrying about whether you are pleasing your partner.

You may feel some resistance to the labels "active" and "passive." Some people feel uncomfortable about being "passive." It is important, however, for each partner to fully experience both roles. If you are a woman having problems reaching orgasm, learning to feel comfortable with the active role will help you. If you are a man having problems with erection, being in a passive role will be a valuable experience for you. Try not to limit yourself to "traditional" male and female attitudes—you may find being in an unfamiliar role quite enjoyable.

Self-pleasuring and Selfishness

Many of us have negative feelings about the word "selfishness." We may have been told that we were selfish when, as children, we wanted to do things which gave us pleasure. However, many people with sexual problems are actually too "unselfish." From trying to give too much, they have lost the ability to enjoy their own feelings.

Think of your behavior in sexual encounters on a continuum from "selfish" to "unselfish." Some of you may be more toward the unselfish end—a little more concerned about your partner's enjoyment and satisfaction than about your own enjoyment.

In the early exercises, I will ask you to move more toward the "selfish" end of the continuum, in the sense of concentrating on your own feelings without worrying about your partner. When you are in the active role in each exercise, touch your partner for your own pleasure and for no other reason. Touch and caress strictly for your own enjoyment and do not consider at this point what types of touches or caresses your partner might prefer. Find what pleases you.

You may notice that this advice goes counter to what is recommended by the authors of many highly regarded books on sexuality. They recommend that the sensate focus caresses be done with the goal of pleasing the partner. In fact, some authors refer to the sensate focus roles as that of the "pleasurer" and "pleasuree," or "giver" and "receiver."

I have found that this orientation toward the exercises *increases* anxiety and performance pressure. In my experience, encouraging clients to touch for their own pleasure has brought nothing but positive results, while allowing a client to attempt to "give me pleasure" generally results in increased pressure to perform, increased anxiety in the sexual situation, and a shutdown of arousal.

It is normal and loving to want to please your partner and to want to know that your partner is enjoying himself or herself. Learning to focus on your own sensations and your own enjoyment will actually make you *more* sensitive to your partner's needs and feelings in the long run. Knowing what you enjoy will make it easier to communicate those things to your partner. Learning to concentrate on and enjoy your own sensual and sexual feelings when you are the passive partner will give you the confidence that your partner enjoys the same freedom when you are active.

The Here and Now

Suppose you are a man whose face is being caressed. Your partner is caressing your face in a way that feels good for her. She is not taking into account what you like or what might feel best for you. Suppose that she caresses your whole face once or twice and then lingers on your forehead for what you perceive to be a long time. If you have thoughts such as, "I wish she'd go back to my chin," or, "I wish she would hurry up and touch my ear—that would really turn me on," or even, "When are we going to have sex?" then you are failing to concentrate fully on your experience of the present. When you realize this, you must consciously *will* your attention back to the point of contact between your skin and your partner's skin.

Sex, like life, happens in the here and now. Dwelling on thoughts of your sexual problems in the past will distract and depress you. Speculating about what will happen in the future (even a few seconds into the future) will make you anxious. Stay in the here and now!

Sexual Arousal

Let's say that you are caressing or being caressed and you are thinking, "This feels good, it feels relaxing, but it's just not turning me on. Something must be wrong." Relax. It's not supposed to be turning you on.

Men, you are not expected to get an erection during the sensate focus exercises. Many men do not get erections during a hand caress, face caress, back caress, front caress, or even a genital caress. Women, you are not expected to experience vaginal lubrication during these caresses. If you *do* experience sexual arousal, that's fine. You may notice a momentary twinge in the groin area, a feeling of wetness, or the presence of a half or full erection. Return your attention to the area that your partner is touching or that you are touching. Do not focus on the genital area unless that is the area being touched.

If you feel aroused, do not try to make it "better" by squirming around or rubbing against your partner. On the other hand, do not do anything to push your arousal away or contain it in any way, either. It is perfectly acceptable to feel sexually turned on during the exercises, but it is not *necessary* to be turned on in order to learn from the exercises.

Summary ...

Before going further, you may want to review the main points we have covered:

1. Always focus on the point of contact where your skin touches your partner's skin.

2. When you are active, do the exercise for your own pleasure and do not worry whether your partner is enjoying it. Use a slow, light caressing technique.

3. Stay passive when in the passive role.

4. Stay in the here and now.

5. Focus on sensual pleasure rather than sexual arousal.

Chapter 3

❤

Common Sexual Problems

In this chapter I will describe common sexual problems in terms of how they are experienced. I also list the various psychological terms associated with them. This will enable you to define any special concern you may have. But remember that labeling problems is not as important as becoming aware of your body....

My orientation is toward the self and a personal experience of sexuality. Throughout the book I define sexual problems and states of healthy sexual expression in terms of the *individual's* feelings and reactions.

Some therapists view sexual problems as aspects of a relationship, and will only treat a couple as a unit. Certainly there are cases in which both members of a couple have sexual problems, and other cases in which a person may cause a sexual problem in his or her partner. In my view, however, sexual problems are not always a sign that a couple has a dysfunctional relationship.

While sexual feelings and sexual problems arise in interactions with other people, I believe sexual functioning and sexual healing ultimately lie within the self. In fact, many sexual problems have their roots in people allowing others to define their sexual feelings for them. *You* must be the judge of what feels good to you and what your experience is. Using this program, you can learn to define and experience your own sexual feelings before you interact with a partner.

You will find that I define sexual problems rather broadly. It is my impression that a great many adults in our society feel some level of anxiety, discomfort, or insecurity about sexual activity. Because the mind and the body function together, it follows that if you *think* you have a problem in the area of sexuality, even a small amount of worrying about it may become a problem in itself. The worry can distract you during sexual activities and can dull your sexual arousal.

My primary training is in helping people who have psychologically-based sexual problems—problems that are learned, rather than those caused by some physiological injury or disability. I have included information in this book on how to determine whether a problem is psychological or physical.

Sexual Problems in Women

It is common for women to be **unable to reach orgasm.** Psychologists refer to this condition as "inhibited female orgasm." Older terms include "inorgasmia," "anorgasmia," or "preorgasmia."

Some women may never have experienced orgasm. Others may be able to reach orgasm—even multiple orgasms—through masturbation but not through intercourse. Some may have been able to reach orgasm through intercourse in the past but can no longer, or are orgasmic with one partner but not another. Some women who are able to reach orgasm feel they are trying too hard or taking too long. Still others realize that as they approach orgasm they consciously shut down, or wish they could experience multiple orgasms.

The exercises in this book are intended for women who have experienced orgasm at least once. "Orgasm" is defined here as the combination of rhythmic contractions of the pelvic muscles and the psychological feeling of release. If you do not know what orgasm feels like, I suggest you gain some preliminary experience and knowledge before starting this program. I recommend *For Yourself* by Lonnie Barbach for assistance in learning to masturbate to orgasm. In addition, many feminist health centers offer women's orgasm groups in which other women will show you how to masturbate to orgasm. Your gynecologist may also be able to recommend a source of preliminary orgasm training.

Surveys on human sexual response indicate that many women either do not have orgasms at all, or do not have them during intercourse. In some cases, studies they have read or heard about may have convinced some women that they are unable to have orgasms. Certain temporary physiological states can also interfere with the ability to reach an orgasm. For example, alcohol and certain prescription and nonprescription drugs may temporarily dull sexual arousal.

I believe that, in the absence of nerve damage or other physiological injury or defect, any woman can have an orgasm. If you can reach orgasm through masturbation, you can also do so through intercourse, because this means your body is physically capable. If you can have one orgasm through intercourse, you can have as many as you want through intercourse.

Inability to experience an orgasm during certain activities probably has more to do with the nature of the activities than with any deficiency on the woman's part.

There are many sites in the female genital region in which an orgasmic response can be triggered; in Part III I have described activities that provide strong stimulation to these areas.

If you have experienced a problem reaching orgasm, here are some of the questions you should ask yourself. Do you feel your partner is pressuring you to have an orgasm? (It may be more than just a feeling—he may actually be pressuring you.) Do you feel defensive if your partner asks, "Did you have an orgasm?" Do you feel there is something wrong with your body and the way it responds sexually? Do you feel you may not be built like other women? Are you distracted during intercourse by thoughts such as, "I wonder if I'm going to have one this time"? Do you engage in frenzied activity during intercourse such as vigorously rubbing your clitoris rather than slowly and sensuously enjoying the feelings of intercourse? Do you get close to an orgasm with a partner and then feel yourself shut down? Do you let your partner define whether or not you have had an orgasm without correcting him if he is wrong? Do you allow your partner to continue activities that bother you or that you do not enjoy? Do you fake orgasms?

In order to reach orgasm through intercourse whenever you want to, you will have to make some changes! You must take responsibility for the fact that you are not reaching orgasm now. You will need to learn to stimulate yourself to orgasm before you can show your partner how to do it. If your partner has been pressuring you, you will have to bring this issue out in the open. You may need to discard stereotypes about women's roles during sexual activity and adopt positions that are stimulating rather than "ladylike." You can learn how to communicate with your partner explicitly during sexual activity, even if this seems embarrassing for you now.

Making these changes may not be as difficult as you

think. Many problems with orgasm are not caused by any deep-seated psychological conflict but by simply not knowing how the body works. Many women do not explore their own bodies until after they have been with sexual partners. If you do not know how your own body works, you may be unable to withstand real or imagined pressure from your partner. You may believe that you cannot have an orgasm, or feel discomfort with the sexual interaction in general. Remember that biological or physical causes for the inability to reach orgasm are very rare!

How long should it take to reach orgasm during intercourse? This is for you to decide. I will teach you techniques of arousal that are so effective that you can reach orgasm immediately upon penetration if you want to.

> *Carol,* the client of a male surrogate partner, is an example of a woman who was experiencing problems in becoming aroused to orgasm. She had experienced orgasms in the past and could reach orgasm through masturbation.
>
> Carol's problem was that as she approached orgasm during intercourse, she felt herself shutting down and becoming distracted. In work with a surrogate partner she revealed that she had severe psychological conflicts related to a recent incestuous relationship. Every episode of intercourse brought back the anxieties associated with that relationship. For Carol, successfully dealing with her sexual problem required a combination of talking about the incest episode with her therapist and working with the surrogate partner on the distractions and anxiety as they occurred in sexual situations.
>
> Carol also began to understand that she had

spent so much time worrying about other people's enjoyment and doing what other people wanted that she had forgotten it was all right to accept her own sexual desires and enjoy herself. The turning point came for her in an exercise with the surrogate partner in which he did nothing unless she specifically asked for it. Today, Carol regularly experiences orgasms during intercourse.

❤

The **inability to become sexually aroused** at all is another common problem among women. Psychologists call this "female sexual arousal disorder;" it may involve the failure to lubricate, or it may be no more than a lack of sexual pleasure or excitement.

If you have felt sexual arousal in the past, you can feel it again. If you have never felt sexual arousal, you can learn to feel it. There are many reasons why you may not be feeling it now. You may be bored or you may lack sexually arousing activities. The most common reason is that anxiety overwhelms you as you start sexual activity. Remember that anxiety is both physical and mental— manifestations of anxiety include rapid heartbeat, perspiration, and muscle tension, as well as thoughts of worry or distress. Remember that our bodies are set up in such a way that we cannot be both anxious and aroused at the same time. To overcome sexual anxiety you must learn to recognize it and train your body to relax.

> *Donna's* problem with sexual arousal stemmed from several sources. She was somewhat bored with her husband, who was rather mechanical about sexual activity and tended to prefer positions that were not very stimulating for Donna. She went through a stage of apathy toward sexual activity and then began to feel apprehensive

whenever she thought her husband might want to have sexual intercourse. This apprehension increased until it prevented her from becoming aroused at all.

Donna's problem was treated in an unusual way. She and her husband entered sex therapy together, and each worked with a surrogate partner. Donna's male surrogate partner trained her to recognize her anxiety and to relax so that she could learn to become aroused again. Her husband's female surrogate partner showed him how to avoid pressuring Donna and how to use more stimulating sexual positions. The supervising therapist later assigned Donna and her husband sexual exercises which they practiced together to improve communication between them and to provide more stimulating sexual experiences.

❤

A third, less frequent, female sexual problem is **vaginismus**—a reflexive tightening of the muscles around the opening of the vagina that makes penetration by the penis impossible. It is usually obvious what the problem is, but a very inexperienced person might be confused. A woman who has vaginismus may learn to avoid penetration by sliding up on the bed to get away from the penis or by clamping her legs shut.

There are different degrees of vaginismus. Some women experience it only in response to attempts at insertion of a penis. Others may not be able to insert anything in the vagina, not even a finger, a tampon, or a Q-tip. Vaginismus may occur with one partner but not with others. It may also be accompanied by muscle tightness in the stomach, thighs, and buttocks.

If you have vaginismus, you may have experienced it in various ways. You may think that your partner has an exceptionally large penis or that you are "very tight." You may think, "I just can't do it" or, "It just won't go in, no matter how hard I try" or even, "I want to do it, but I'm just not big enough."

Vaginismus is *not* related to the actual size of the vagina. It is rare for a vagina to be so small that it will not accommodate a penis, no matter how large. Vaginismus often develops in response to sexual trauma, for example, rape or molestation, or painful intercourse. It is common for women who develop vaginismus to do so as a defense against pain, especially pain that was never properly diagnosed or treated. Vaginismus may also develop in response to a partner who thrusts too hard or for too long, causing discomfort or pain. Women sometimes develop vaginismus in response to a partner's sexual problem—for example, women whose partners have problems with erection or ejaculation may develop vaginismus. Vaginismus can also lead to sexual problems in the partner; for example, a man may develop premature ejaculation in response to a partner whose vagina is always tightly shut.

Many sex therapists treat vaginismus with a series of dilators, or rods of increasing width, which the woman inserts. I recommend rather, as detailed in Part II, that you begin with learning to relax and then insert first your own fingers and then those of your partner before you attempt to insert a penis. Above all, you should be the one who controls all insertion.

With vaginismus, it may be more important than with other sexual problems to determine the underlying causes of the condition. If your vaginismus is caused by a sexual trauma, you need to deal with that trauma, and should seek a qualified therapist. Your fear and anxiety stemming from trauma or pain in the past can be overcome, and the sexual exercises in this book can help with the vaginismus.

To overcome vaginismus, you can learn to exercise and control the muscles around your vagina, to relax your stomach and thigh muscles and focus on sensations in your genitals, and to touch your own genitals and masturbate to orgasm with or without the insertion of objects in your vagina. You and your partner can learn to communicate honestly with each other about the fear and frustration you have both been experiencing, and develop trust in each other.

Sally developed a typical case of vaginismus in response to molestation as a child for which she had never received any help or treatment. Before marriage she feigned a number of illnesses in order to avoid intercourse with her future spouse. In twenty-five years of marriage, she had fewer than ten successful episodes of intercourse ("successful" defined here as including penetration; she found no enjoyment in any of these instances and in fact felt them to be quite painful). Her husband developed a severe case of premature ejaculation and sought extramarital relationships in which he eventually had successful and satisfying intercourse.

Unlike the examples of Carol and Donna, Sally's case does not have a happy ending. Her husband begged her to accompany him to therapy, but she refused to admit there was anything wrong with her. Her life is frustrating and depressing, and unfortunately there are thousands of women like her. But many other women in Sally's situation have obtained help and overcome vaginismus, and now enjoy pain-free and satisfying sexual expression.

Sexual Problems in Men

The most common complaints reported by men involve **problems with erections.** Psychologists include a range of these complaints in the term "male erectile disorder," an older term for which is "impotence."

Some men report they have never had an erection in their lives. Others have erections through masturbation but never with a partner. Still others had erections in the past but do not have them now. Even more common are: Having an erection with one partner but not others, having an erection but losing it before penetration, having an erection but losing it some time after penetration and before ejaculation, having an erection only during a certain portion of sexual encounters, having an erection but feeling that it is not hard enough, or having an erection but continually worrying about it.

Why go into so much detail? In order for you to deal with your problem, you must learn to know your body well enough to determine at which stage of the sexual response cycle your response shuts down. You also need to determine whether your problem is to any degree physical.

The experts are uncertain what proportion of problems with erection are physical and what proportion are psychological. Clearly, problems due to nerve damage or vascular damage are one hundred percent physiological. Other problems may be caused by a combination of physical and psychological factors. Remember that the mind can be responsible for changes in the body, so almost every erection problem has some psychological component.

A few simple self-tests can help you decide whether your problems are physical or psychological. Do you have erections when you masturbate? On a scale of "1" to "10," with "1" being no erection and "10" being an extremely rigid erection, how hard are the erections you have with masturbation? If you can have a fairly strong erection with masturbation, there is probably nothing physiologically wrong with your penis, and any difficulties you experience with a partner are likely to be psychological. There is a good chance the exercises in Part III will help you.

You may be unable to answer the previous question if you do not masturbate. Do you wake up with an erection in the morning? On a scale of "1" to "10," how hard is it? It is normal for healthy men to have three to four erections of different hardness per night during periods of dream sleep. If you do not know if you have erections during sleep, ask your partner to stay awake for part of one night to find out. If you have erections during sleep or upon waking, your penis clearly is capable of becoming erect. The erection exercises in Part III will enable you to have erections reliably.

If you do not have erections with masturbation or when you sleep, there is a chance that your problem is physical. I have already mentioned nerve damage, which may be due to diabetes or other causes. These problems may be permanent, but other physical problems are definitely temporary. For example, some drugs which are routinely prescribed for ulcers or high blood pressure may cause temporary but emotionally devastating erection problems. Nonprescription drugs such as antihistamines can temporarily interfere with erection, and cigarette smoking has recently been found to do so. It is well known that alcohol consumption, especially to excess, interferes with erection.

If you think there is a chance your problem may be physical, you should consult a urologist who specializes in erection problems to see what your treatment options are. Be aware, though, that I have seen many clients who had been told by urologists that their problems were physical. In some cases the urologist had even recommended a penile implant. These clients chose to try psychological sex therapy first, and in most cases it worked! My impression is that psychological problems are much more common than physiological erection problems.

You should also keep in mind that after age twenty-five or thirty, the erection response tends to decline. It may take longer to have an erection, and the erections may not be as hard as they used to be. This is normal (although it does not happen to all men) and to my knowledge there is nothing that can be done about it. And the old cliché, "Use it or lose it," *does* apply to male sexuality. If you do not masturbate or have intercourse or otherwise regularly allow yourself to go through your whole sexual response cycle, from stimulation to erection to ejaculation, your body can forget how to do it. However, if you had erections and satisfying sexual activity at some time in the past, you can probably learn to do so again.

I had a client in his sixties who had not had sexual intercourse or masturbated to orgasm for twelve years. Nevertheless, after less than one year of sex therapy, he is currently having strong erections several times a week and satisfying intercourse at least once a week. I worked with another man in his seventies who had not had sexual intercourse for over twenty years, and who had not masturbated or had morning erections in twelve years. His erection response began to return after several sessions of sex therapy.

If your problems with erection are primarily psychological, they can easily be treated by the program described in this book. Ask yourself if you are experiencing the following feelings: Do you have a performance orientation toward sexual activity rather than a pleasure orientation? Do you often use the words "perform" or "work" or "success" to describe sexual activity? Is pleasing your partner more important to you than your own enjoyment? During sexual activity, do you obsessively wonder whether your penis will stay hard? For you, does "sex" equal "intercourse," with any other activities only secondary to the "main event"? Do you pressure yourself to have an erection and wonder what your partner will think of you if you don't have one? Once you get an erection, do you engage in a frenzy of activity in order to "use it before you lose it," rather than taking the time to enjoy the sensuous feelings in your body? Do you feel that your partner is pressuring you to get an erection? *Is* your partner in fact pressuring you?

In my work as a surrogate partner, I have heard many clients say these things—and I have seen the same clients learn to rid themselves of these thoughts and obtain erections with ease. Ridding yourself of problems with erections will mean making some changes in your life, however. You can learn to focus on your own feelings rather than on your partner's responses. You can learn to accept stimulation to your body. You can learn to trust your feeling that you are hard and cease comparing your erection with any external standard of performance you may have imagined. You can learn to stop thinking of sexual activity as a performance. You can learn to admit that it is panic that you feel when your erection starts to go down, and you can learn to remedy the situation.

> *Larry's* story illustrates a typical progression from perceived erection failure to anxiety to actual erection failure. At first he noticed that sometimes he would lose his erection during intercourse with his wife. Then he found he had a difficult time having an erection at all. Soon he began to avoid any type of sexual activity or touching because of the anxiety he would feel.

After about a year he entered therapy. He followed the program I will describe in Part III and regained the ability to have intercourse with his wife. Their sex life now is better than ever. Larry learned in therapy how to reduce the anxiety he felt during sexual encounters and how to cope with changes in his sexual response as he aged. He learned to relax his body and allow his natural sexual response to happen instead of increasing his anxiety by "working at" getting an erection.

❤

A second common sexual problem for men is **premature** or **rapid ejaculation,** which, like so many sexual problems, can be a matter of degree. Some men ejaculate with no physical or sexual stimulation at all. Others ejaculate when a woman rubs against them. (This may be a reflex ejaculation that occurs without the pleasurable feeling of orgasm.) Some men ejaculate upon being touched with a hand or mouth, and some ejaculate immediately upon penetration. It is very common to ejaculate a few seconds after penetration.

Some men experience premature ejaculation only the first time they are with a new partner. Others ejaculate quickly during a first episode of intercourse, but last much longer if they have intercourse again during the same sexual encounter. Premature ejaculation may occur with any type of stimulation or it may be specific to the vagina.

Premature or rapid ejaculation is not defined by the amount of time or the number of thrusts before ejaculation. Premature ejaculation is defined by the *feeling* that you do not have control over when you ejaculate.

A major cause of premature ejaculation is anxiety. It is almost never caused by a physical problem. You may not feel as if you are anxious—or you may panic at the thought of any sexual encounter. Either way, your body has learned a response in which your tensed muscles, irregular breathing patterns, and distracting thoughts are triggering your ejaculation. By learning to recognize both your level of anxiety and your level of arousal, you will find you can last as long as you like.

If you have been experiencing a problem with rapid ejaculation, you may feel as if everything on your body is connected to your genitals. A kiss or touch anywhere on your body triggers a genital response and accompanying panic. You may try to ignore your genitals and think of something else. You may find yourself masturbating several times a day in order to wear down your arousal level before you attempt intercourse. You may worry constantly that you are not satisfying your partner and that she is going to leave you, and you may try to make up for your premature ejaculation in other ways in the relationship. When you are close to ejaculation, you may feel "Oh no!" rather than pleasant anticipation.

Very severe premature ejaculation involves ejaculating with any kind of stimulation prior to penetration. Other cases are less severe. If you simply ejaculate sooner than you want to when inside the vagina, your problem may be only that you are not having sexual intercourse often enough. Consider your body and how often you spontaneously have an erection and feel like ejaculating. If you do so daily, but have intercourse only twice a week, you may find that with more frequent intercourse you will not be ejaculating as soon. You might try having intercourse as many times as you would like to for a few days to find out what the optimum frequency is for you.

To eliminate a more severe problem of premature ejaculation, you can learn to *focus* on sensations in your genitals, rather than ignore them as you probably have been doing. You can put priority on your own sexual response, rather than on your partner's response. You can learn that ejaculating is wonderful whenever it happens, rather than something to be avoided. You can learn to relax your body so that you fully experience and enjoy your ejaculation and no longer feel your body to be out of control.

One of my clients, *Robert,* was married for a number of years to a woman who constantly belittled him, but for whom he cared a great deal. After every sexual encounter, she would tell him that he had failed to satisfy her. He began to last shorter and shorter lengths of time during intercourse, and eventually to ejaculate before penetration. His wife had a number of extramarital affairs and told him all the details, including how well her various lovers had satisfied her and how long they had lasted. Eventually she refused to allow Robert to have intercourse with her at all.

Robert tried to make up for his perceived inadequacies in other ways, such as buying his wife gifts. I say "perceived" inadequacies, because when he entered therapy after starting divorce proceedings, he found that after experiencing the program described in this book with a cooperative partner he had no problems at all in lasting as long as he wanted. Robert's case illustrates how a partner can contribute to sexual problems. Chances are that Robert would never have developed premature ejaculation if his partner had not exploited his self-doubt. In any event, he went on to a satisfying second marriage.

Albert had one of the most severe cases of premature ejaculation I have ever seen. Albert ejaculated at a mere touch anywhere on his body, and had done so for over twenty years. Through the program I describe in Part III, he learned to maintain intercourse for up to half an hour. He spent almost a year in therapy, but for a case of such severity and duration, his progress was truly remarkable.

❤

A third problem often experienced by men, **inhibited ejaculation**, (also called retarded ejaculation or ejaculatory incompetence) is the inability to have an ejaculation at all. Again, the problem may be one of degree. Ejaculation may be altogether inhibited, or, more commonly, the man may be able to ejaculate when he masturbates but not during intercourse.

In my practice, I have noted two specific types of inhibited ejaculation. Some men experience difficulty ejaculating due to their having worked to control their ejaculations, generally over a period of years. In other words, they tried to avoid premature ejaculation and overdid it. Dealing with this type of problem is a relatively straightforward matter, for which the program described in Part III works very well.

In other cases, the man developed the ejaculation problem as a result of anger against women or a specific woman. This anger, which may be of long duration, destroys the intimacy in the relationship. While the man may maintain an erection indefinitely, his feelings are so dulled that his penis has literally "numbed out." This more severe and, usually, long-standing form of inhibited ejaculation may also respond to exercises similar to those I describe, but the process may take several years. In general, if a man has ever been able to ejaculate in the vagina during intercourse, he can probably learn to do it again. If a man has never been able to ejaculate in the vagina, the outlook is somewhat less positive.

An inability to ejaculate may also be caused by consumption of alcohol or some drugs. It can be a sign of a medical problem such as an enlarged prostate. You should check with a urologist if your inhibited ejaculation problem began rather suddenly.

If you are experiencing inhibited ejaculation, you may have some of the following experiences. You may accept that you have a problem but rationalize it by saying, "Well, most women like a guy who can last a long time." You may even be proud of yourself for lasting longer than you perceive other men are lasting. You may have intercourse steadily for hours and yet still have to leave the room and masturbate in order to ejaculate. You may feel that you have lost sensation in your penis and that it is no longer a part of you. You may or may not be aware that you are angry, and you may be unaware of the source of the anger you feel.

If you are experiencing the first type of inhibited ejaculation I described (holding back), it should be a fairly easy and enjoyable process for you to relearn how to ejaculate during intercourse, though it may take a few months. If you are experiencing the type of inhibited ejaculation related to anger, you may need to consult a qualified therapist to help you deal with the psychological aspects of the problem.

For example, you will have to confront the fact that, while some women enjoy prolonged intercourse, few women like intercourse without intimacy, and that may be what they have been experiencing with you. You will have to confront the fact that instead of thinking what a great lover you are, the women you have been with may have been thinking, "Isn't he ever going to come?" If you are willing to confront and deal with these issues, you have an excellent chance of learning to experience intimacy, learning to feel your body again, and learning to ejaculate during intercourse, though you may require the help of a qualified therapist. You will have to decide whether ejaculating during intercourse is worth truly sharing yourself with your partner in such intimate behaviors as kissing, talking, and passively accepting stimulation by your partner.

In my experience, this type of inhibited ejaculation is the most difficult sexual problem to deal with. In fact many clients quit therapy rather than face up to their problems. For some men, not being able to ejaculate is preferable to experiencing vulnerability and intimacy. But if you are motivated to deal with your problem and are willing to do the sensate focus exercises in this program, your chances of learning to ejaculate with a partner are good and the outlook is positive.

Don's inhibited ejaculation was of the first type that I described, the result of holding back ejaculations for a number of years to avoid impregnating his wife. In therapy Don learned sexual activities that promote intimacy, such as kissing and sharing feelings; he learned to relax his body when he felt close to ejaculation and began again to feel sensations in his penis.

Steve had a more severe problem, worsened by other factors in his relationship with his wife. He had never forgiven her for an extramarital relationship she had in the early years of their marriage, and his inability to ejaculate with her dated from that time. By the time he sought sex therapy more than twenty years later, his wife had refused to have sexual relations with him for five years, and she had developed a number of psychosomatic illnesses. Steve had developed problems with erection in addition to ejaculation. However, he could masturbate to ejaculation in front of a partner, and there was an excellent chance that he could have learned to ejaculate again during intercourse. But he decided to quit therapy, saying that sex with his wife was just not worth being intimate with her in other ways.

❤

A fourth problem men can experience is **flaccid ejaculation,** in which the man ejaculates while the penis is still soft. It is not uncommon for men occasionally to experience flaccid or reflex ejaculation. Chronic flaccid ejaculation is fairly rare, and little is known about it; alcohol use may be a factor. Flaccid ejaculation combines problems of erection and premature ejaculation, but I usually treat the premature ejaculation first and then concentrate on the erections. As with any problem with erections, you should determine whether it has a physiological cause.

> I have seen only a few instances of flaccid ejaculation. In *Bruce's* case, I attributed his sexual problems to his extremely poor health habits (especially his drinking and smoking) and his debilitated physical condition. Over a period of three months, in about twelve sessions, Bruce learned to control his ejaculations and to have erections more than sufficient for penetration, despite apparent and probably irreversible damage to his arteries.

Problems Common to Both Sexes

Both men and women may feel a **lack of sexual desire,** sometimes referred to as "hypoactive sexual desire disorder" or "inhibited sexual desire." According to many sex therapists, this is the most common sexual problem in America today. It is almost always transitory, a result of stress or overwork. There is nothing wrong with you sexually if you feel no desire when you are tired and overworked! If you have felt desire in the past, you can feel it again—if you take the time. Following the program in Part II will almost certainly restore your feelings of sexual interest, just because committing yourself to the program will force you to set aside time for yourself.

In a less common but more severe case of inhibited sexual desire, a person may say that he or she is just not interested in sex. It is actually very rare for a person to feel no sexual desire whatever. The person who says that he or she is not interested is more likely to mean that he or she is not interested in doing a particular activity with a particular person at a particular time (for example, intercourse, with you, right now).

You do not need to feel any sexual desire or arousal to do any of the exercises described in this book. You only need a willingness to spend time touching. "I guess I'm just not interested in sex" may have been a good enough excuse for avoiding sexual activity with your partner in the past, but it is no reason for avoiding the exercises I will describe. Doing the exercises *will* increase your level of desire, so if you would like to feel more sexual arousal than you currently do, this program is likely to help you.

An expressed lack of sexual desire may in fact be more accurately explained as a desire discrepancy—one partner desires sexual activity more often than the other. The range of what is normal as far as sexual frequency is concerned is broad. One person might like sexual activity many times a day, while another may feel desire only a few times a year; both are quite normal. But it can become a problem if long-term partners have discrepant desire patterns. If your partner feels low sexual desire and is not interested in treatment, you will have to decide whether you want to stay with a person who does not want to attempt to feel greater sexual interest in you.

Often, people who feel they have no desire simply suffer from lack of knowledge or inexperience. They have never engaged in activities that were really stimulating and memorable. This program includes a range of such activities that you can try.

Finally, there is the rare case in which an absolute lack of sexual feelings is caused not by fatigue, repression, or inexperience, but by physiological problems such as an absence of the necessary hormones or brain damage. Of all the clients with whom I have worked, I have only seen one person who manifested no sexual interest at all.

❤

Sexual phobia, or **sexual aversion disorder,** is a common problem for both men and women. Symptoms include racing heart, sweating, muscle tension, and feelings of panic during a sexual encounter or when thinking about a sexual encounter. In extreme cases there may be nausea, vomiting, or diarrhea. Although this sounds alarming, in my experience this problem is one of the easiest and fastest to treat, and using the basic sensate focus exercises in Part II should help greatly.

The strategy is to follow the exercise instructions exactly, with the added agreement that whenever you feel the least bit of anxiety you will let your partner know and back up to a previous exercise with which you are comfortable. Through these exercises you will deal with your anxiety on the physiological level, bypassing the mental components of anxiety. Since sexual phobias as well as other phobias are *learned* fears, you can learn *new* body responses to situations that currently trigger anxiety.

Alan had a fairly strong phobia about sexual activity. He became nauseous at the thought of intercourse and suffered incapacitating stomach cramps. I would have accomplished nothing trying to talk him out of feeling that way. Instead I used exercises similar to those I describe in Part II to teach him to relax his body. He did so well that he quit therapy after only a few sessions, confident that he could approach his girlfriend without the old panicky feelings.

If you do the exercises described in this book consistently, you can heal erection, orgasm, ejaculation, or anxiety problems, and become sexually functional.

The exercises can also be used for other conditions that indirectly affect sexual functioning. For instance, you might try the program if you are experiencing changes in your body's sexual responsiveness due to aging or illness. As the exercises emphasize knowing your own body and your individual response, rather than comparing yourself to some external standard, you are likely to find them a help in adjusting to change. Men who have had prostate surgery or major cardiac surgery may feel unsure of their sexual abilities. They may hesitate to initiate sexual activity for fear they may not have an erection, or they may be afraid to exert themselves. The exercises described in this book, being relaxing rather than stressful, provide a gradual and nonthreatening way to reintroduce sexual expression into your life after surgery.

I have worked with many clients with chronic health problems such as muscular diseases. One client in particular stands out in my memory. *Darryl* had cerebral palsy and used a wheelchair. He had little voluntary control of his arm and leg muscles, and speech was quite difficult for him. He felt sexual desire and was able to masturbate to ejaculation. He was curious to learn how much he could do sexually and was able in therapy to experience a full range of activities, including body caressing, oral sex, and intercourse.

❤

You might start with the exercises in this book if you have no sexual experience at all. The exercises start at a very basic level and you need no prior sexual experience with a partner in order to do them.

The exercises may also help you develop sexual confidence if you are feeling some degree of insecurity due to a recent life change such as divorce or marital separation. If you have difficulty concentrating during sexual activity and find your mind drifting off, you should find this program extremely helpful. Or, if you feel you have no problems at all, but would simply like to enhance one or another area of your sexual feelings or sexual activity, you will find the program rewarding. These exercises will enable you to start over sexually with increased arousal and intimacy.

Part II

❤

The Sensate Focus Program

Chapter 4

❤

Exercises to Do by Yourself

Now that you have a clear understanding of the aspects of your sexuality you wish to enhance, and you know the basic principles of the sensate focus program, you are ready for some exercises that will teach you more about your body and its natural sexual response. These are sensual and sexual exercises that you should practice by yourself before you go on to the exercises to be done with a partner. They include breathing, control of the pubococcygeus and pelvic muscles, self-caressing, "peaking," and "plateauing." *You should do these exercises no matter what area of your sexuality you want to work on.* They will give you a real sense of the importance of some of the basic concepts we have already discussed. Even if you decide not to do the rest of the program, you should do the exercises in this chapter to learn more about what you enjoy and how you like to be touched.

The exercises are not tiring, and you do not need to be in especially good physical shape to do them. However, if you have any physical problem or are being treated for any condition, please check with your physician before trying any of the exercises here. If at any time during an exercise you experience any pain, discontinue the program immediately until you can see a doctor.

Exercise 1: Breathing

Before you do anything else, you need to make sure that the way you are breathing is relaxing you and not making your sexual problems worse. There are two aspects of breathing you should pay attention to. The first is *slowness*. Slowing your breathing will in turn relax your whole body. The second is *evenness*. Keep your breathing consistent and even in order to allow sexual energy to flow throughout your body. Holding your breath when you become sexually aroused will actually diminish your arousal.

To start, lie comfortably on your back with your clothing loosened. Place your hand over your heart to get a sense of how fast it is beating. You do not need to time it. Now place your hand on your abdomen. Blow all the air in your lungs out through your mouth. Slowly breathe in through your mouth, and then immediately, but slowly, exhale. Pause several seconds between exhaling and inhaling. Do not pause between an inhalation and an exhalation—in other words, do not hold your breath in. The inhale/exhale movement should be one continuous process. Lie quietly and breathe like this, slowly and evenly, for a few minutes.

If you are especially anxious, or have a lot of stress in your life, also try the following breathing exercise. Blow all of the air out of your lungs through your nose rather rapidly. Now take all the air you can back in through your nose, *slowly*. Think of it as caressing the inside of your lungs with the air. Relax your stomach muscles. As soon as the air is all in your lungs, start breathing it back out, *slowly.* Don't hold your breath at all.

Your breathing is now under your conscious control. Do this five or six times. It will slow down your heart rate and lower your blood pressure. This simple breathing exercise, done regularly, can give you all the relaxation that you need to do the exercises in this book.

Exercise 2: The Pubococcygeus Muscle

The pubococcygeus muscle ("PC muscle") is in fact a group of muscles, which run from the pubic bone to the tailbone and support the pelvic floor. In women this band of muscle surrounds the opening of the vagina, and in men it surrounds the base of the penis. In women with vaginismus, this is the muscle group that spasms and prevents penetration. In men, this muscle can spasm and bring on a premature ejaculation. In both sexes, this muscle contracts and flutters during orgasm.

Identifying and exercising the PC muscle group is extremely important, because many sexual difficulties can be traced to problems with this muscle. First we will learn to identify the muscle.

Women, to locate your PC muscle, place one of your fingers inside your vagina up to the first knuckle. (If you have vaginismus, just place your finger on your vaginal lips.) Pretend you are urinating and you want to stop the flow. The muscle that you feel tightening when you do this is the PC muscle group. Make sure you are only flexing that small muscle and that you are not tensing your abdomen or thigh muscles at the same time. You should be able to move your PC muscle without it being visible to anyone looking at you.

Men, to locate your PC muscle, lightly place one or two fingers behind your testicles. Pretend that you are urinating and want to stop the flow. The muscle that you feel tightening is the PC muscle. You may notice that your penis and testicles "jump" a little when you flex the PC muscle. Your abdomen and thigh muscles should not be tensing at all. You do not need to have an erection to exercise your PC muscle.

Now that you know where your PC muscle is, here are the exercises I want you to do: Three times a day, flex the PC muscle twenty times. You can do this while driving your car or brushing your teeth!

There are two common mistakes that people make when beginning these exercises. The first is to overdo the repetitions. Like any other muscle, the PC muscle can become sore.

The second mistake is to fail to isolate this small muscle group from nearby larger muscles. Your abdomen, thighs, and buttocks should not move at all when you exercise the PC muscle. If you really have trouble with tensing other muscles, overwork those muscles first so they do not interfere. For example, if you tend to tense your abdominal and stomach muscles when you try to do PC exercises (as many men who are experiencing premature ejaculation tend to do), consciously tense and untense those stomach and abdominal muscles ten or twenty times before you begin your PC exercises. That way the stomach and abdominal muscles will be fatigued and will not interfere with your PC exercises.

You do not need to keep your finger on the muscle as you exercise it—you will be able to feel it move internally. If you find that you are having trouble isolating the PC muscle, keep your finger on it the first few times you do the exercises.

Do not hold your breath as you do these exercises. Just breathe normally and regularly. Repeat this first simple PC muscle exercise three times a day, every day for three weeks.

Then, in addition to twenty quick repetitions, I want

you to add ten slow repetitions. You should be able to feel your PC muscle slowly suck in and then slowly push back out. Try to tense the muscle for five seconds, hold for five seconds, and then push back out for five seconds. The first time, you may only be able to do this once or twice. Try to eventually work up to ten repetitions, each taking five to ten seconds. It may take you some days or weeks—that doesn't matter. Don't push yourself. There is no world class "PC muscle-building" championship that I know of.

(When I was training to become a surrogate partner, we compared PC muscle strengths by means of a liquid-filled meter with a tube that we inserted in the vagina. After inserting the cylinder, you would push down on the muscle and the liquid would go up on a scale. We were not concerned about getting up to some absolute level of strength—we just used this gadget as a novelty, and this is a point I want to stress. Avoid developing a performance attitude toward any of these exercises.)

The important thing for you to learn here is to locate your PC muscle group and regularly exercise it. You may design your own PC exercises and add them to the ones I have suggested. You can do them to music, just like aerobics. Find a level of PC fitness that is comfortable for you, and then maintain it for the rest of your life.

Some sex therapists believe the PC muscle has been overrated and is unimportant in sexuality, while others of us swear by the PC muscle. I ask all of my clients to do PC muscle exercises because I have seen incorrect use of the PC muscle associated with so many sexual problems, including erection problems, vaginismus, and premature ejaculation.

In my experience, correcting poor PC habits can often help resolve a sexual problem without any further sex therapy. An example of someone with poor PC habits is a man who consciously or unconsciously flexes his PC muscle as he is starting to feel an erection response. At that early stage of the arousal cycle, flexing the PC muscle will force blood back out of the penis and will result in loss of the erection.

Even if you do not have a sexual problem, exercising your PC muscle can help you because it increases the area in the pelvis to which blood can flow during sexual arousal. This can increase enjoyment at all stages of the sexual response cycle, including orgasm.

In women, a strong PC muscle can tighten the vagina. In both men and women, flexing the PC muscle at the moment of orgasm can often intensify the orgasm. Men with control of their PC muscle can have multiple orgasms. A strong PC muscle also means better bladder control. In fact, these exercises were first developed by an obstetrician named Kegel to control incontinence in pregnant women and women who had just given birth; they are often called "Kegel exercises." And besides all of the reasons given above, doing the exercises is fun and feels good.

I cannot stress the importance of PC exercises too much. In therapy, the clients who learn most quickly to have orgasms, control their ejaculations, or have erections are those clients who were consistent about exercising the PC muscle. Exercising your PC muscle every day for the rest of your life can prevent physical and sexual problems.

Now that you know how to exercise your PC muscle, I am going to tell you something which may surprise you—don't use it. I *do* want you to do the specific exercises I have just described for this muscle, but I do *not* want you to use the muscle during any sensual or sexual activities described in this program without specific instruction. Contraction of the PC muscle at the wrong time can decrease arousal, and its correct use will not be explored until the advanced portion of the program. So for now, learn to identify it, isolate it, exercise it—and leave it alone.

Exercise 3: Pelvic Thrusts and Rolls

People who are experiencing sexual problems often unconsciously tighten the muscles in their pelvic area. The next two exercises are for your abdomen, buttocks, and thigh muscles, and will help loosen you up and release the tension from those areas.

Pelvic "thrusts" can be done either lying down or standing. The idea is to rock or tilt your pelvis from back to front without moving any other parts of your body. It is especially important to keep from tensing your stomach muscles or leg muscles.

If you are lying down, put your knees up and rock or tilt your buttocks slowly up and down so they are the only part of you that moves off the floor. Do it as quickly or slowly as you like and as many times as you like. Do it to music if you want to, or vary the speed. The important thing is to keep all your other muscles relaxed and to keep your breathing regular—again, do not hold your breath. To make sure your breathing is correct, you may find it helpful to grunt or make some other noise with each lift. If you want to do pelvic thrusts while standing or walking, simply stand and rock your pelvis back and forth or, as you walk, consciously thrust your pelvis forward with each step.

Pelvic "rolls" are similar to thrusts: Again, either lying down or standing, move your hips sideways in a continuous rolling motion. Think of Elvis Presley. If you have difficulty getting the knack of this movement, buy a hula hoop and practice with that. Practice rolls at different speeds. Especially practice doing them as *slowly* as you possibly can. Combine thrusts and rolls and do them to music if it feels good. Try to do a series of these thrusts and rolls for about ten minutes every day. Close your eyes so that you can really feel your body. Enjoy yourself. And remember to keep the muscles in your buttocks, leg and abdomen relaxed. Men especially tend to have tight hip muscles. Learning to loosen them up can often increase your ability to become sexually aroused.

In my experience, most people are able to do pelvic thrusts and rolls without risk, especially if they do them slowly. However, if you have back problems, especially in the lower back, consult your physician before attempting them.

A number of other physical exercises can be beneficial to your sex life, particularly those that involve stretching, squatting, or spreading the legs. In general, any sport or physical exercise should benefit your sex life, simply because, as I discussed in Chapter 1, physical well-being improves our mental health.

Exercise 4: Self-caressing

To learn how you would like to be touched, and in preparation for the sensual exercises you will do later with your partner, I would like you to practice sensual caresses on yourself. Remember that the emphasis is sensual, rather than sexual. By learning to simply touch yourself in a relaxing, gentle way, you will lay the foundation for all the exercises that follow.

You may feel a little self-conscious caressing yourself, especially when you move to the genitals, and especially if you have never touched your genitals in this way before. That is fine. Practicing the self-caress will make you more comfortable. It is very important to learn about your own body response in order to increase your ability to become aroused.

Choose a small area of your body, such as your arm, your chest, or your thigh, for your first self-caress. Put some lotion on your hand and slowly touch yourself. *Focus on the point of contact between your hand and your body.* If your mind wanders off to something else, bring it back to exactly how your skin feels. Touch yourself slowly and lightly—do not massage the muscles. Touch only the skin. Notice the temperature and texture of your skin. Think about what you feel right now, rather than anything you have been taught or remember from the past. If you have trouble concentrating, slow your touch down. Use more lotion if your skin feels dry. Spend ten to fifteen minutes doing this, learning the feeling of your hand against your skin.

Now try a genital caress. This is very different from masturbation. You will not try to turn yourself on or have an orgasm. You will learn what kind of touch you like on your genitals.

Women, lie down or sit naked in a comfortable position. Use some baby oil or other lubricant on your fingers and begin slowly to touch your inner thighs and your genital lips. If any part of your body is tense, make a conscious effort to relax it.

This caress may include only the outer genitalia, or you may put your fingers all the way inside the vagina. Concentrate on the touch exactly the way you did when you caressed part of your body in the previous exercise. If your mind starts to wander off, slow down the movement of your hand and consciously bring your mind back to that point where skin is touching skin. If you become sexually aroused, that is fine, but that is not the goal. The only goals are to enjoy yourself and learn about your own body.

Try different touches. Touch yourself the way your partner usually touches you and the way you usually touch yourself, and then touch yourself in a completely different way. Do not spend any more time on the clitoris than you do on the other parts of the genitals. Relax all your muscles and keep your breathing even. If you have an orgasm, fine. Do not try to make it happen, do not try to make it better, and do not try to push it away. Do not tense up against it, just experience it.

If you become aroused, make a conscious effort to relax your muscles and take a deep breath. Gently, slowly, stroke yourself to get the maximum sensual awareness and enjoyment. Concentrate on changes in texture, temperature, and arousal as you touch different areas. Continue for about fifteen minutes.

Men, sit or lie naked in a comfortable position. It will be important for you to remember that this is not the same as masturbating. The purpose of this exercise is not to have an orgasm but to learn what type of touch feels good on your penis and scrotum.

Use some baby oil or lotion if you like. Slowly begin to stroke your penis and scrotum, concentrating on the texture and temperature of your skin. *Keep your attention on the exact point of contact between your fingers and your genitals.* If your mind wanders off, slow the movement of your hand and bring your mind back to the touch.

Experiment with different types of touch. Touch yourself the way you usually do, the way your partner usually does, and in new ways. Keep all the muscles in your body relaxed and breathe evenly. If you feel yourself approaching orgasm, do not do anything to make it happen, make it better, or push it away. Just allow it to happen. Continue for fifteen minutes.

❤

Practice each of these self-caressing exercises at least once, but preferably a few times, before you begin the exercises with your partner. Repeat them as many times as you like—you will find that they are a good way to relax. The important things are to concentrate on the touch and to avoid feeling any pressure to become aroused or have an orgasm. Caressing yourself like this will teach you to pay attention to touch, breathing, and muscle relaxation—the three most important aspects of arousal.

Exercise 5: Arousal Awareness and Peaking

You are now ready to learn a process called "peaking." Here you allow yourself to reach a certain level of arousal and then come back down. Before you learn to "peak," however, you must be able to recognize how sexually aroused you are.

To develop arousal awareness, think of your sexual arousal on a scale from "1" to "10," with "1" being not aroused at all, and "10" being orgasm. For men, it is important that you notice how aroused you *feel,* regardless of how strong your erection is. You can learn to recognize feelings of arousal internally or emotionally without having to look at your erection.

The following guidelines may help you recognize how aroused you are. At "2" or "3," you would feel mild twinges of arousal, but arousal is not really constant. Level "4" or "5" would be a constant low arousal, and levels "6" to "7" steady moderate arousal. At "6" or "7," you are starting to feel that you would like this exercise to continue. At "8," if you had to talk, you would sound somewhat out of breath. Level "9" is the feeling that you are very close to orgasm. Anything beyond "9" is the feeling that orgasm is inevitable.

It does not matter which number you reach on the scale either this first time or any time you do the arousal awareness exercise. What is important is that you start to get a sense of how close you are to orgasm or how far you are from orgasm. If you only reach level "2" or "3," that is fine. If you immediately go straight to "10," that is fine, also. The important thing is that you concentrate on the touch at the moment and let arousal happen as it will, without trying to make it better or push it away.

If you find you have absolutely no sense of how aroused you are and this exercise is frustrating, do not worry. When you do the exercises with your partner, he or she can help you. It takes most people several experiences with this exercise before they are really sure how aroused they are.

The fact that I am asking you to describe your sensual and sexual arousal on a "1–to–10" scale may seem contradictory to what I have said earlier in the book. Please don't get the impression that I am asking you to grade or evaluate yourself—or your *performance* —in any way. The numbers are to help you *describe* your sexual response. For example, reaching a "9" during any exercise is not better than reaching a "3." The idea is not to see how high you can go, but rather to become aware of *the difference in how you feel* at the different number levels. I use numbers because most people understand the concept of a "1–to–10" scale, and find it easy to use.

To begin learning to "peak," repeat the genital self-caress, extending the time to twenty minutes. Start to give numbers to the different states of arousal you feel. Every five minutes or so, ask yourself, "Where am I now?" Do not try to reach any particular state of arousal. Caress yourself the same way you did before, during the genital self-caress.

The second time you do this exercise, talk to yourself a little differently. Ask yourself, "When do I feel I am at '4'?" and then find that point. "What does '6' feel like?" and then find it. And so on.

During this arousal awareness exercise, continue to caress yourself in the way you have been practicing. Keep your attention focused on how your skin feels, and allow your awareness of how aroused you are to come and go as it will. Focus on the touch. Relax. Breathe. Keep your body as still as possible. If you have an orgasm, try to experience it without moving your body or tensing up against it. Now, open your eyes and take a deep breath.

The third time you do this exercise, try to bring your arousal up to a peak and then allow it to go back down. To begin, relax, breathe, and caress yourself as you did in the two previous exercises. When you feel you are at "5," stop caressing, and note that your arousal goes down a couple of notches. Then caress yourself again until you feel you are at "6." Allow yourself to go back down again. Remember to keep your caress as slow as possible, and focus on the touch. Try for "7," "8," "9," and "10." Spend about five minutes on each peak, including both the up and down phases.

In the peaking process, the phase in which you allow your arousal to go *down* is as important as the phase in which it goes up. Feelings (or emotions) of all kinds can be defined as *changes* in body states and mental states. We perceive feelings to a large degree in terms of *contrast.* Letting your arousal decrease and then allowing it to come back up provides the contrast you need in order to be able to recognize how aroused you are.

Allow yourself plenty of time for the arousal to go down, even though you may be tempted to forget about the exercise and go all the way to orgasm. When you begin to caress yourself for each new peak, be sure to start slowly.

If you have vaginismus, problems reaching orgasm, or problems with erections, you may not be able to go all the way to "10." This is fine. Do not push yourself or work at it. The important thing here is to be aware of—and *enjoy*—exactly what you do feel, without putting any pressure on yourself.

If you have a problem with premature ejaculation, do this exercise very slowly, making sure that your stomach, thigh, and buttocks muscles are relaxed and that you are breathing evenly. If you have a problem with inhibited orgasm or ejaculation, emphasize slowness and concentrate intently on how your skin feels. If you are having erection problems, concentrate on your feelings of arousal rather than monitoring your erection. If you have anxiety about sex in general, be sure that your breathing is slow and even and that your muscles are not tensed.

If you are a woman who has difficulty reaching orgasm, or a man who ejaculates quickly, I would suggest that you do this exercise (or the plateauing exercise that follows) at least twice a week through the remainder of this program. You may want to continue it anyway, as it feels good and is a pleasurable alternative to masturbation.

❤

It is possible for a man to "over-peak." After more than three or four peaks at very high levels you may find yourself temporarily unable to ejaculate. This is nothing to worry about. Just stop the exercise at "9," and your ability to ejaculate will return in about ten minutes.

Do this peaking exercise several times a week until you are able to recognize with some degree of confidence how aroused you are. You do not have to reach orgasm every time or, indeed, any time. When you begin to touch yourself, notice whether you feel like having an orgasm or not. Do not try for one, but do not push it away if it happens. If you do have an orgasm, keep your body as relaxed and motionless as possible so that you can feel what happens in your body when you have the orgasm.

It is possible to go all the way through your sexual response cycle to orgasm without moving. If you feel an orgasm approaching, take a deep breath and open your eyes. Being able to experience an orgasm while remaining completely passive will be tremendously helpful in enhancing your sexual enjoyment and in solving sexual problems, as it will help you learn to focus totally on all of the body sensations that happen during an orgasm.

Exercise 6: Plateauing

Plateauing is very similar to peaking, but here the focus is on maintaining a certain level of arousal. It begins with the genital self-caress. Focus on the touch, relax, and breathe as before.

Pick a comfortable level at which you would like to stay for a while. I suggest "6" to begin. When you reach "6," stop the caress and let yourself go back down, but only to "5." Then take yourself up to "7." After a while, see if you can pick out the finer points, such as "5½" or "6½." Hover around the "6" level by adjusting the speed of your touch or your breathing.

There are many ways you can maintain yourself at a given level of arousal. Change the area you are caressing or the pressure you are using during the caress. For example, a man who would like to remain at "7" could either slow down his caress or move from touching the head of the penis to touching the scrotum. When he feels the arousal go down to "6," he could then begin to touch himself with more pressure or touch his penis near the head. A woman who wanted to remain at "7" could caress her clitoris until she reached that point and then slow down and move the caress to the inner lips.

The plateauing technique is a way for you to learn to play with your arousal. By plateauing and remaining aware of how aroused you are, you can test and practice different types of stimulation. This awareness of your own arousal levels and the many different touches you can use to arouse yourself will also help you be more sensitive to your partner's arousal when the two of you begin to do exercises together.

This exercise will also help you fine-tune your response. Try plateauing at "7," "8," or even "9" if you feel comfortable with it. The key is to relax at the same time that you are stimulating yourself. Practice will allow you to maintain yourself indefinitely at an extremely high level of arousal when you are with a partner.

"Plateauing," because of all the numbers involved, may sound a bit complicated as you first read about it. Remember, however, that you already have a lot of experience recognizing your arousal levels. You already know how easy and relaxing it is to allow your arousal to go up and down. This is a key concept I hope you will keep in mind—you are allowing arousal to happen to you in a natural and relaxed way, rather than "working on yourself."

Chapter 5

❤

Performance Anxiety

You now have some experience practicing sensate focus caresses on your own body. When you were alone, you probably did not worry much about how you were "performing." Before you move on to doing sensate focus exercises with your partner, I would like to give you some ideas on how to deal with any performance pressure or anxiety you might feel in the new situation.

In our society, we tend to view sexuality—and much else—as a performance: We wonder constantly if we could "do it better." We also tend to think of a sexual problem as something "missing." In fact, as I have said, if you experience problems with your sexuality, you probably need to *subtract* stress or anxiety, rather than *add* props such as X-rated videotapes, exotic clothing, or other erotica.

Our society overemphasizes a visual-logical-verbal processing of sense information. These sensate focus exercises will return you to the tactile-emotional way of receiving and expressing information about your world that you used naturally when you were a child. The exercises will also help you become acquainted with your partner on a body level as well as a mental level.

Anxiety

Most if not all sexual problems are anxiety-related. In problems with erection and vaginismus, for example, the anxiety hits at the beginning of the sexual encounter. With inhibited desire and sexual fears, the very thought of the encounter provokes anxiety. In premature ejaculation, inhibited ejaculation, and the inability to reach orgasm, anxiety enters at various points in the encounter.

How to reduce and eventually eliminate sexual anxiety is one of the most important things you can learn from this book. The sensate focus exercises are designed to teach you, step by step, how to identify and deal with anxiety during the course of a sexual encounter.

If you have been experiencing sexual anxiety for a long time, even the earliest sensate focus exercises may have made you anxious. Do not blame yourself for this. Even fairly mild levels of anxiety take time and practice to overcome completely, as you work to undo the results of years of fearful reactions to sexual encounters.

Remember, though, that the exercises will not help you if you remain anxious while you do them. You will do yourself more harm than good if you attempt to disguise your anxiety just to get through an exercise. It is *extremely* important that you stop any exercise that makes you anxious; if you continue you will only be reinforcing your fear.

Signs of anxiety include cold hands and feet that do not warm up, tensed muscles (especially in the thighs and abdomen), rapid shallow breathing, fast heart rate, a feeling of nausea or nervous stomach, and racing thoughts or inability to concentrate on the exercise. This anxiety should lessen with continued slow, nonthreatening touching.

There are three steps to dealing with the anxiety you may feel before or during an exercise. First, bring your focus back to the touch. Use the concentration on the touch to occupy your mind. Second, breathe properly. When you become anxious, you hold your breath or breathe too shallowly. Take deep breaths that you can feel all the way down in your stomach. Third, consciously relax your thigh, stomach, and buttocks muscles. Even momentary tightening of those muscles can cause anxiety and interfere with your natural sexual arousal response.

If your anxiety persists, tell your partner that you feel uncomfortable and back up to an earlier exercise that you were able to do comfortably. Only after you feel relaxed with the earlier exercise should you add in elements of the new exercises.

❤

You will also want to know how to respond if your partner becomes anxious during an exercise. When you are the active partner, you will be touching your partner in a way that feels good for you, and spending most of the time focusing on your own feelings. However, you should be able to notice if your partner is anxious or tense. Obvious signs of anxiety include rapid shallow breathing, a jumpy or quivering stomach, and muscle tension in the thighs and abdomen.

If you notice any of these signs in your partner, slow your touch down. Continue to caress as slowly as you can. If signs of anxiety do not go away, encourage your partner to take deep breaths. If necessary, stop the exercise and back up to a previous exercise with which you both felt comfortable.

Your passive partner may tighten up his or her leg muscles, especially during caressing of the genital area. This muscle tightening is a learned habit that causes sexual problems and makes them worse. For example, in men who have problems with erection, tightening these muscles "steals" blood away from the penis. In men with premature ejaculation, tightening these leg muscles and the PC muscle can trigger the ejaculation. In men and women who have difficulty reaching orgasm, tightening the leg muscles can actually prevent orgasm.

If you notice your partner tightening his or her legs, give the legs a very light tap or pinch to remind your partner to relax those muscles. If you notice yourself tightening up when you are in the passive role, consciously relax your legs. Tightening the leg muscles is a habit that is very easy to break. Three to five instances of your partner reminding you to relax will usually take care of this habit.

❤

Some people experience severe forms of anxiety, called panic attacks, panic reactions, or phobic reactions. (A phobia is a learned irrational fear, such as fear of heights, fear of being in enclosed spaces, or fear of snakes.) You may have a phobic reaction to the whole idea of sexual contact, or just to some element of the sexual encounter.

Signs of this kind of severe anxiety reaction include: profuse sweating; paleness; an extremely rapid heart rate; breathing difficulties; a feeling of tightness in the chest; and nausea, vomiting, or diarrhea. These sensations are usually accompanied by a feeling of extreme dread or even the feeling that one is about to die of fright.

Psychologists have made great strides in the treatment of phobias, and even this very severe type of anxiety is usually completely treatable. I have successfully used the sex therapy program outlined in this book to treat sexual phobias. However, if your sexual anxiety is quite severe, you should seek the assistance of a qualified therapist.

The treatment usually used for phobias is called "systematic desensitization," which is not unlike the treatment of allergies. The phobic person is presented with the feared stimulus in a very mild form, and then in increasingly stronger forms, while being trained to relax. Because your body cannot be relaxed and anxious at the same time, as we have learned, you gain control of your anxiety by consciously promoting relaxation. And if you are gradually taught to respond in a relaxed way to a fear-producing stimulus, this relaxation response will carry over to other fear-producing situations in your life. (This approach is also called "in vivo" desensitization, which means, in real life situations. Some programs train people to relax while imagining scenes of sexual activity, but I have found these less successful than relaxation training in the actual sexual situation.)

In a similar way, this program offers a series of sensual exercises that gradually become more sexual. The first few exercises are nonsexual and nonthreatening. You are simply training your body to relax. By the time the exercises become more sexual, this relaxation response should be established, and you should be able to respond to a sexual situation with relaxation rather than anxiety.

The process I recommend has much in common with that described by Herbert Benson in his book *The Relaxation Response.* According to Benson, four things are necessary for the relaxation response to occur: A mental device, quiet, a comfortable position, and a receptive or passive attitude. In the exercises that follow, focusing on the sensation of "touch" provides the device that keeps your mind occupied. You will take a passive role during part of each exercise, and you should do your exercises in a quiet room and a comfortable position. I suggest you choose a room that is free from distractions. Do not even play soft music in the room. Music can be added after you have learned to focus, but during the early exercises it will distract you. In order to maximize your sense of touch, close your eyes for at least part of each caress.

Learning how to decrease your anxiety by sustaining the relaxation response helps more than your sexual functioning. It will also benefit your physical and mental health in general.

Performance

Men, particularly, tend to think of a sexual encounter as a "performance." A man might say, "I was with a woman, but I was unable to perform," meaning, of course, that he failed to have an erection. Thinking of sex as work or as some kind of performance put on for the benefit of the partner (or for persons who are not present) is an attitude that can only detract from the enjoyment of a sexual encounter.

In most areas of life we are trained to achieve. For example, those who work hard and succeed on the job and at school are valued in our society. They are the "go-getters," the "self-made" successes. And from childhood on, we are encouraged to compete, an attitude which often helps us achieve work or school goals (although possibly at the expense of our mental health).

Sexual activity, however, is an area in which this performance orientation has only negative effects. For example, men who have been successful in work often encounter difficulties with erections as they age. Success in business often means thinking many steps ahead of what you are doing in the present. In sexuality, thinking ahead leads to feelings of anxiety and pressure to perform, which result in "erection failure."

The use of "active" and "passive" roles in the sensate focus exercises is designed to make it difficult if not impossible for you to maintain a performance orientation toward sex. There is no point in "working at it" if you know your partner has been instructed not to provide any feedback. The person in the active role has no real choice but to act for his or her own enjoyment.

As you do these exercises, watch yourself for signs of performance orientation. If you catch yourself thinking, "I tried so hard, but the exercise just didn't come out right," recognize that you are looking at the activity as a performance situation.

Stop trying. Clear your mind. Experience yourself, rather than judge yourself. Your sexual response will happen normally if you relax and give yourself plenty of time.

Don't hurry through these exercises. You have been conditioned by the culture to believe that moving quickly wins you the most rewards. But if you rush through this program, you will not learn what you need to learn from each exercise and you will have to repeat each exercise more often. Paradoxically, the more slowly you proceed with these exercises and the less you plan or think ahead, the sooner you will find that your problem is a thing of the past. You will benefit more if you start this program with the thought, "I will have fun and enjoy myself," rather than, "I will get better—or better at *it*—as soon as possible."

Learning to relax during sexual activity and ceasing to view sex as a performance will also benefit other areas of your life. Clients often report to me that sensate focus techniques help them concentrate in other areas, such as studying, or listening to music, or cooking. Other clients say they are actually more productive at their jobs because they concentrate on the task at hand and no longer make themselves anxious by thinking ten steps ahead.

Pressuring Your Partner

I have suggested several ways to stop putting pressure on yourself to perform sexually. However, your sense of being pressured to perform may not be imagined. For example, if your partner says things to you like, "Did you come yet?" "Are you close?" "Why aren't you hard yet?" "Can't you last longer?" or even, "I want you to come now," you are justified in feeling that you are being pressured.

If you are in the habit of saying things like this to your partner, please stop. If your partner does this, ask him or her to please stop. You may not have realized that these simple statements and questions can create tremendous psychological pressure. After each sensate focus exercise in the book there are guidelines for giving feedback: constructive, positive, and pressure-free ways for both partners to communicate feelings about their sexual activities.

While direct and overt performance pressure is fairly easy to recognize, pressure conveyed through nonverbal cues may be more subtle. Picture a sexual experience in which everything seems to be going fine, in the sense that both persons are functioning well and doing activities they feel they *should* enjoy. Yet for some reason both feel uneasy. They may start to search for something to which they can attribute their negative feelings: "I must be in a bad mood," or, "I guess I'm not feeling sexy." What is most likely is that they have become caught up in a widening spiral of interpersonal performance expectations, each picking up that the other is thinking or worrying, rather than enjoying the experience.

Let's say that a man is giving an oral genital caress

to a woman. If he is enjoying himself and concentrating on exactly what he is doing (in other words, if he is focused on the sensations), then the woman is free to enjoy herself and focus on her pleasure also. However, if the man thinks, "I wonder if she's enjoying this?" or, "I wonder how much longer I'm going to have to do this until she has an orgasm?" the woman will pick this up.

Your partner cannot read your mind, but your partner can tell if you are concentrating on what you are doing and if you are enjoying it. We may not know exactly what is going on, but we realize something is not right, because we feel uncomfortable. In fact, we are picking up our partner's nonverbal cues, which are more honest than the actions taking place. We may attribute the feeling of discomfort to, "Something is wrong with me or with my response," when we need to recognize that there has been a subtle shift in the quality of the encounter. What will happen in the situation I have just described is that the woman will think to herself, "Uh-oh, he's expecting me to have an orgasm pretty soon. I better fake it." At this point, the sexual interaction becomes based on expectations, worries, and performance pressures, rather than sensate focus and mutual enjoyment.

In another example, a woman might be caressing the genitals of a partner who has difficulty having an erection. Instead of enjoying what she is doing and concentrating on how her hand feels on his genitals, the woman may think—briefly—"I wonder when he's going to get hard." Her partner will instantly pick up on the fact that something is not right: The quality of her attention has changed. He may then think, "Uh-oh, she's getting tired, she's getting bored, why am I not getting hard?" Needless to say, if this situation isn't remedied, his problem will only become worse, as the performance anxiety will begin earlier and earlier in the sexual encounter.

Another source of pressure is the idea that you are

somehow responsible for your partner's enjoyment. You need to take responsibility for your own arousal and enjoyment, and learn to please yourself while accommodating your partner's needs, so that you can become aroused together.

How do you avoid this pitfall of unwittingly putting pressure on your partner or of succumbing to pressure put on you? First, become aware of the problem. If you feel pressure, any pressure, this means that the pressure is real. At this point it doesn't matter what *caused* it— you just need to get rid of it. If your first reaction is to think, "There is something wrong with me," redefine the feeling as, "I am feeling pressured due to something that is going on in this situation." Then you can see the solution: To make sure you truly enjoy what you do by doing only what you enjoy. By practicing the sensate focus techniques, you will learn what you enjoy. Staying focused on what you do will increase your enjoyment, and your enjoyment will leave your partner free to enjoy also. If an activity or situation is so uncomfortable that you cannot focus on it, stop and turn to something with which you feel comfortable.

Spectatoring

"Spectatoring" is thinking when you should be feeling or experiencing. An example would be a man who is receiving a genital caress and thinks as his partner's touch moves toward his penis, "I wonder if it will get hard. It's starting to feel a little hard now. I bet it won't get very hard. Uh-oh, it's going down now."

Spectatoring does not mean literally watching your performance with your eyes, but being unable to put a stop to obsessive thoughts about one's response. Women, especially those who have difficulty reaching orgasm, can also be prone to this type of thinking.

An example might be a woman who is receiving a

genital caress. As her partner moves closer to the clitoris, she thinks, "I wonder if I'm starting to lubricate. It feels a little wet down there. I wonder if I'll have an orgasm this time." As the stimulation becomes more enjoyable, her thoughts switch to, "I'm getting kind of close. I wonder if I'll have one this time. Wait, now it's slipping away. Damn, it was so close!"

Spectatoring tends to be a concern in men with erection problems and women who have a problem with orgasm. It rarely occurs with premature ejaculation, since the ejaculation is often over before the man has time to think about it.

The cure for spectatoring is additional practice with sensate focus techniques—in fact, over-practice. If your mind is totally focused on the touch, you will be unable to comment internally on your "performance." Practicing sensate focus will help you learn the difference between *focusing* on your response and *worrying about it*. If spectatoring is a severe problem in any given exercise, back up to a less threatening exercise where it is easy for you to pay complete attention to the point of contact between your skin and your partner's skin.

Trust

For people with long-standing sexual problems, sex can become something they avoid in thought and conversation as well as behavior. They often find it difficult to trust a partner, especially if the problem (such as vaginismus) originates in a trauma such as incest or rape by someone who was trusted. Often, a person who experienced sexual trauma at an early age went on, naively, to attempt to deal with the problem by initiating sexual activity too soon or persisting in unhealthy sexual experiences which only increased their lack of trust.

The sensate focus exercises can help to build trust between partners, in that each exercise has limits and ground rules to which you should adhere.

For example, the face caress calls for touching only the region from the top of the head to the base of the neck. It is not uncommon in my experience for men to exceed the boundaries of this exercise by touching the breast. When this happens in my practice, I ask the client to please stay within the bounds of the exercise. Why? Obviously, I like to have my breast touched as much as anyone else, so why not let him do it? After all, it might give him an erection, which is what we're working toward in the long run....

Staying within the limits of the exercise, and holding the other person to them, helps to develop *an atmosphere of trust* in which both partners know what to expect and know that the other is trying to help create a good experience. If my partner pushes the limits of an exercise, I know that he is not totally focused on the touch, and this also distracts me from being able to focus one hundred percent on the touch.

Say that a couple agrees to a face caress for ten minutes each. As the man is caressing the woman's face, he moves down to touch her breast and soon she reaches back to stroke his genitals, and before you know it, they are having intercourse.

Going beyond the exercise in this way is not a major issue if both persons are free of sexual problems and are using the sensate focus exercises primarily to increase the pleasure in their sex lives. But here is what will happen for couples with sexual problems. They will not learn what the exercise is designed to teach, that is, how to touch and be touched in a *sensual* manner. They will learn instead that every touch leads to sexual activity. This will reinforce the anxiety or performance orientation which was their problem to start with.

To get the most from the sensate focus exercises, stay within the limits of the exercises. For the first few exercises (unless otherwise specified), do not go on to genital contact or sexual intercourse either during or after the exercise. You will only undo what you have learned in the exercise.

Sex therapists differ about whether you should continue having intercourse or doing the other sexual activities you were used to while you go through a sex therapy program. You will have to make your own decision. I recommend you avoid following a nonsexual exercise with sexual activity. Take a break first, or you will reinforce in your mind the idea that sensual touching is always followed by sexual activity.

Use your feelings as a guide. If you feel any doubt about doing a sexual activity that you have not yet reached in the sensate focus exercises, it is best to hold off. However, if both you and your partner feel totally comfortable with continuing to do sexual activities even without, for example, orgasms, go ahead.

Whether you continue having intercourse during the program will also depend on the nature of any problem you may be working on. Obviously, a man who cannot maintain an erection would not be able to, but a man with inhibited ejaculation would. I discuss these issues more specifically in Part III. If you feel you cannot stay within the limits of the exercises, you should not do them. To add more sexual contact than instructed during an exercise will do you and your partner more harm than good. Not only will you fail to benefit from the exercise, you will have taught your partner that you are untrustworthy, whereas if you adhere to the limits, you will build trust. Trust can help you rid yourself of a performance orientation toward sexual activity.

Feedback

Each exercise concludes with a feedback discussion. You should speak openly and honestly. Many couples with sexual problems have learned to be dishonest with each other about their sex lives. An example would be a woman who continually fakes orgasms. You may feel embarrassed to admit that you have lied to your partner or withheld the truth, perhaps for many years, but your joint decision to finally do something about your problem should give you the confidence to start responding honestly.

The exercises will not do you any good if you lie about your feelings. For example, please do not tell your partner you enjoyed the exercise if you didn't. Please do not tell your partner that you were able to concentrate if you weren't, just so you appear to be doing things correctly.

After each exercise I list questions you can use as a guide for your discussion. Here is a sample of these questions, and a few comments:

How comfortable was each partner with the active role? With the passive role? Were each of you able to remain completely passive? If you felt uncomfortable with either role, you should repeat the exercise until that role becomes comfortable and natural for you.

What part of the time were you able to fully concentrate on sensations while you took the active role? The passive role? Ideally, you should feel you are concentrating on the touch most of the time, but the actual amount of time you are focusing is not as important as learning to recognize when you are distracted and bringing yourself back to the touch. If you have trouble focusing in either role, you need to practice the role until you are able to concentrate more fully.

Some people raise objections at this point. "These exercises are too boring and repetitive. There's no way I can focus on touching for twenty minutes." What can I say? Learning a new behavior requires three things: actually doing the behavior, finding the behavior in some way rewarding, and *repeating* the behavior. If you feel bored, you are not focusing on the point of contact between your skin and your partner's skin. The way to relieve your boredom is to consciously will yourself to pay attention to your practice of the exercises.

It is natural for extraneous thoughts to intrude—out of nowhere you may start to think about the kids or your job. This distraction is different from boredom and is nothing to worry about. Simply catch yourself and bring your mind back to the touch. You will know that you were totally focused on the touch if after an exercise you feel that it was too short or that the time passed much more quickly than you expected.

When you were active, how much of the time did you do the exercise for your own pleasure? How much of the time were you trying to please your partner? Did you worry whether the passive person was enjoying the caress, or did you wonder what he or she was thinking about? If you really focus during the active role, thoughts about your partner should not enter your mind. The exception would be if you can see by outward physical signs that the passive partner is extremely anxious and is not relaxing.

When you were in the passive role, did the touch feel like a caress or like a massage? Was it mechanical? Did you feel pressured to respond? If your touch is perceived by your partner as being rough, fast, or mechanical, you may need to adjust your caressing technique.

Did either partner experience sexual arousal during the exercise? If you experienced arousal, did you try to get rid of it, try to make it better, or just leave it alone? It may make it easier to talk about arousal levels if you use a numerical scale, as in the self-caressing exercises.

Did each person follow the instructions for the exercise, or did one or both partners attempt to go beyond the limits? Did each person feel that the exercise was in general a positive experience? Was either partner working at it (trying to please, or trying to get aroused)?

After each exercise, each partner should report on his or her anxiety level during the exercise, and his or her perception of the partner's anxiety level. You may want to use a scale of "1" to "10" to help you talk about anxiety, with "1" being no anxiety and "10" being extreme anxiety.

You should repeat an exercise if either partner experienced high anxiety which did not go away, felt unable to concentrate most of the time in either role, felt pressured to respond, or failed to adhere to the limits of the exercise.

Setting a Schedule

Improving your sex life, enhancing your relationship with your partner, overcoming sexual fears and problems—all these require a commitment of time. Some sex therapy programs ask both partners to make a contract to do certain exercises at certain times. You and your partner will need to decide how often you want to do the exercises. If you tend to disagree about things, or have difficulty remembering schedules, a written agreement may help. It is my experience that it is much better to do the exercises at prearranged times rather than to wait until you "feel like it."

I recommend setting a schedule at the start of each week and then sticking to it. The ideal would probably be two or three sessions a week. One exercise a day is too much—your mind and body need time to internalize changes—but you should do an exercise at least once a week to maintain continuity. I go into this in more detail in the section in Part III on "Developing Your Personal Program."

Summary ...

Before turning to the exercises, I want to review the main points we have covered. Actually, this review is so important, I call it "The Sensual Mindset," and have repeated it as Appendix I so you can find it easily. I suggest you go back to it again and again until the ideas in it become second nature to you.

1. Always focus on the point of contact where your skin touches your partner's skin.

2. When you are active, do the exercise for your own pleasure and do not worry whether your partner is enjoying it. Use a slow, light caressing technique.

3. Stay passive when in the passive role.

4. Stay in the here and now.

5. Focus on sensual pleasure rather than sexual arousal.

6. If anxiety does not quickly decrease after the first few minutes of an exercise, ask your partner to go back to a less advanced exercise.

7. Don't work at it.

8. Agree on the limits of the exercise beforehand and do not go beyond those limits.

9. Provide honest feedback after the exercise.

To sum up still more concisely: Focus on the touch, breathe evenly, and relax your muscles.

Focus, breathe, relax.

Chapter 6

❤

Session 1: Spoon Breathing and Face Caress

The following chapters in Part II contain the basic sensate focus exercises for you and a partner. Each chapter provides descriptions of exercises, possible barriers to doing each exercise, variations, and guidelines for feedback.

The sensate focus exercises described in this chapter are the foundation for the more specific work and concerns discussed in Part III. They should also help in relieving sexual fears, sexual desire problems, and vaginismus.

First, in this chapter, I will teach you a breathing technique which will help you and your partner relax before each exercise. Then you will learn the first sensate focus caress. These are the first two exercises that I do with a client. They are done fully clothed, and they take about one hour. You will need a quiet room, a bed, and some lotion.

Spoon Breathing

You and your partner should lie together on a comfortable bed or couch with one person's back snuggled up against the other person's front. Lie with your legs bent so that you fit together, like two spoons in a drawer. The person who is in back then places his or her hand on the stomach of the person in front. Lie perfectly still and do not talk or squirm around even if you feel yourself starting to become aroused. The purpose of this exercise is relaxation. Pay attention to either your own breathing or your partner's breathing.

Slow your breathing down by taking three or four deep breaths and exhaling forcefully. Make sure that all of your muscles are relaxed by concentrating on each leg and imagining that it is sinking into the bed. Picture your shoulders sinking into the bed also.

This exercise is a prelude to sensate focus work in that you should keep your attention on the overall sensations of warmth and closeness that come from lying next to another person. The breathing is the same type you learned to do in the chapter on self-exercises, only now you are doing it with a partner. Can you become as relaxed as you did when you breathed by yourself?

Spoon breathing may be done clothed or in the nude, but in this first session you should do it with your clothes on. Spoon breathing will help you make the transition from any other activities you were doing into a relaxed, neutral state. Do it before each exercise in this program and alternate being the person in back and the person in front. Do not do this exercise while watching television or doing anything else: Devote your full attention to relaxation and listening to your own body. Do the exercise for five to ten minutes.

Face Caress

The first sensate focus exercise in this program is called the face caress. To do this caress, you will need some type of skin lotion that you and your partner like. You will also need to find a quiet, comfortable room in which to do the exercise. Take the phone off the hook and send the kids to the baby-sitter—you need a room in which you will not be disturbed for forty-five minutes to one hour. You will also need a clock or watch in the room so that you can time the exercise.

The person who will be active first should sit with his or her back against a headboard or wall, with a pillow on his or her lap. The passive partner should lie between the active partner's legs, head on the pillow, face-up. It is important to have the passive partner's face in easy reach of the active partner. This exercise is done fully clothed, but you might want to take off your shoes or belt so that it is comfortable to lie down.

The face caress includes everything from the top of the head to the base of the neck. The active person should begin by taking some of the lotion and warming it up in her hand (let's assume that the woman is the active partner first). Then caress your partner's face. Remember, to caress means to use an extremely slow and sensuous touch. *Touch* the skin, rather than trying to feel muscles underneath the skin.

Slowly move one or both hands across the forehead and down the cheeks. Move across the chin and down to the neck. Don't neglect the ears—many people find touching or stroking another person's ears a very sensual experience. Caress the bridge of the nose, the eyelids, and underneath the eyes. Remember to move as slowly as you can. Continue this caress for fifteen minutes, stop and spoon breathe again, and then switch roles.

You are already familiar with the general instructions for the caresses, but I will repeat them briefly here. When you are the active person, do the caress for your own pleasure. Do not worry about what your partner is thinking or try to do something to make your partner feel good. Your partner will tell you if you do anything that is unpleasant. If your partner does not say anything during the exercise, you may assume that your caress feels good or at least neutral.

What you are learning to do here is to focus as completely as you can on sensations in your skin. Both when you are active and when you are passive, pay attention to the exact point of contact between your skin and your partner's skin.

Because you are probably not used to doing things of this type, you may find it hard to focus at first. Your mind may wander off to work or household tasks. (One thing it should not be wandering off to is whether or not you will be disturbed during the exercise. Make sure that the place you choose to do the exercise is free of distractions. You should feel completely free to lie back and enjoy the exercise.)

If your mind wanders off, this is not a problem. Just recognize that you have become distracted and bring yourself back to focusing on the touch. If you are active, one way to relieve boredom or distraction and focus on the touch is to consciously slow the speed of your caress down by half.

In order to learn to focus as fully as you can on the touch, it is best to cut down on stimulation to the other senses. For example, do not play music in the room while you are doing the caress. Most people find it pleasant to listen to music, but for now we are trying to remove anything that will compete with the caress. You may also want to close your eyes during at least part of the caress in order to concentrate more fully.

Talking is almost always a distraction during a sensate focus caress. If you are passive, the only time you should talk during the caress is if your partner does something that hurts you. If you are active, you should not talk at all, except to say "I'm done now." Don't ask your partner, "Is this okay?" or, "Do you want me to use lotion?" Do what you want to do, and don't worry about your partner. Touch in the way that feels best for you.

When you are passive, your only assignment is to relax and enjoy the way you are being touched. It is not necessary to tell your partner what a great job he or she is doing. Telling your partner how wonderful you feel during the caress or finding some nonverbal way to say it (such as moaning or moving around) will only put performance pressure on your partner.

❤

Here are some issues that commonly come up during this exercise. The first, as I have mentioned, is the problem of distracting thoughts. It is natural to have thoughts about other things during the caress—the important thing is to recognize that this is happening and bring your attention back to the touch.

Sometimes the thoughts will be about the exercises; for example, "I wonder if he's going to touch my breasts pretty soon," or, "I wonder if this will really help my sex life." If you are having thoughts of this type, it means that you are not enjoying what is happening with the caress in the here and now. You are looking into the future or, perhaps, worrying about the past ("Gee, it felt really good when she touched my chin—I wonder if she'll do it again"). The solution for distracting thoughts is to bring your mind back to the touch.

It is also natural to feel some anxiety when beginning the caress. Do not expect to relax completely immediately. It may take several minutes for you to become relaxed enough so that you can enjoy the caress. This is why we do the face caress for at least fifteen minutes each time.

When you are the active person, take just a moment to notice whether your partner seems to be relaxed at the beginning of the caress. Later, notice whether there are any changes during the caress; for example, has your partner's breathing become slower and more regular? This is a sign that he or she is relaxing.

Many people become so relaxed during this exercise that they start to fall asleep. You might find it restful and enjoyable to sleep, but you will not learn anything from the exercise. If you are active and your partner begins to fall asleep, gently wake him or her up.

If you find that the opposite is true, and you just cannot relax during the exercise, tell your partner. Switch roles and see if this helps you to relax, or go back to doing some more spoon breathing. There is no point in continuing the exercise if you are wound up so tight that you cannot relax even when you slow down your breathing, loosen your muscles, and focus on the touch. Stop for now, and come back to the exercise later.

The face caress is an exercise in sensuality, not sexuality. If you become sexually aroused during the face caress, this is fine. If you have an erection and ejaculate, this is fine. Be aware that your arousal is there, but do not try to make it better and do not try to get rid of it or contain it in some way. Focus on the part of your body that is being touched at present, rather than on your genitals.

❤

After the exercise, you and your partner will give feedback to each other about how you felt during the face caress. Use the following questions as guidelines for what to talk about.

When you were passive, were you able to relax totally and not move around? Or did you feel compelled to do something to convince your partner that he or she was doing a good job?

During the active role, did you take pleasure for yourself rather than worry about whether your partner was enjoying the caress? When you are active, you should be able to take pleasure for yourself most of the time.

Which role were you more comfortable with, the active or the passive role? Was it easier for you to focus in one role than in the other?

What part of the time were you able to focus on the touch when you were active? When you were passive? Ideally, you should be focusing on the touch most of the time. If you are not able to focus this much, repeat the exercise as many times as you need to until you are able to do so.

It may be helpful to examine the types of thoughts that are interfering with your concentration. If mundane things intrude, such as the laundry or the shopping list, you probably just haven't had enough practice in focusing—it may take a few more sessions. If you are having thoughts or anxieties about future exercises, this is normal—tell yourself you can worry about these things at some other time, so they don't interfere with your practice.

Did you feel anxious during the caress? Were you able to deal with that anxiety by focusing, breathing, and relaxing? Could you feel yourself becoming less anxious as the caress went on? The important thing is not how high or low your anxiety level was at any point during the caress; the important thing is that you are less anxious after the caress than before.

If you felt sexually aroused during the caress, did you just accept it and keep your attention on where you were being touched, or did you try to make the arousal better, or get rid of it?

Did you enjoy the caress? Did you feel pressured to perform when you were active, or did you touch your partner the way you wanted to touch? When you were passive, did you feel pressured to respond and tell your partner how great it was, or did you feel free to just relax and accept pleasure for yourself?

Was it easy for you to stay within the bounds of the exercise, or did you want to touch areas other than the face? Did you stay within the limits? It is natural to want to continue and do something more sexual, but in order to build trust it is important to do what you both agree to do in the beginning.

Did you have a problem with feeling anxious? If so, you need to focus on your breathing. Did you have a problem remaining passive? If so, you need to relax your stomach, thigh, and buttocks muscles. Did you have a problem staying in the here and now? Did you want to please your partner? Were you working at doing a good job? You need to practice focusing on the touch. Did you have a problem focusing? You may need to caress more slowly. Most of the problems you encounter can be resolved by the three familiar words: *focus, breathe, relax.*

The face caress will help you identify any problems you may be having at a basic level because it is non-sexual and nonthreatening. If you were able to focus and relax, if your anxiety level decreased as a result of the spoon breathing and the face caress, if neither of you felt much performance pressure, and if you stayed within the limits of the exercise, you should go on to the next exercise. If answering these feedback questions pinpointed some problem areas for you, you may want to repeat this exercise until you become completely comfortable with it.

❤

If you are having a *severe* problem focusing on the touch, or you are trying to please your partner, or your anxiety level is staying high, or you cannot relax your muscles, there is another thing you can do. It is called "prescribing the symptom."

The strategy is to figure out exactly what you are having a problem with and then try to do it *wrong*. For example, if you are having trouble focusing, specifically *try* to distract yourself for a few minutes of the exercise. That way, you will know exactly how you feel when you are distracted, and this will provide a contrast for when you actually do feel that you are focused.

If you find that you worry too much about what your partner is thinking, spend a few minutes of the caress actually trying to please your partner, so you know exactly what *not* to do. If your anxiety level is staying high, try to feel as anxious as you can for a few minutes during the exercise! If you are having trouble relaxing your muscles, try to tense your muscles as much as possible.

Doing what you *don't* want to do or feel will highlight what it is that you eventually *want* to do or feel. In addition, it will allow you to feel that you are in control of your sexuality, and it can promote a sense of humor toward your efforts, which is always healthy.

Sequence for Session 1
Spoon breathing — 5 minutes
Face caress — First person — 15 minutes
Spoon breathing — 5 minutes
Face caress — Second person — 15 minutes
Spoon breathing — 5 minutes
Feedback

Chapter 7

♥

Session 2: Body Image and Back Caress

Your second session in this program will include the body image exercise (or body imagery process) and the back caress. This session will take one and a half to two hours. You will need a quiet room with a large mirror, a towel, and some talcum powder.

Body Image

The body image exercise is not a sensate focus exercise. It is a communication exercise or process used to help each person learn to become more comfortable with his or her own body and with the partner's body. In this exercise, you will examine your nude body in detail in front of your partner, and tell your partner what you like and don't like about your body. You will also discuss whether certain parts of your body have positive or negative feelings associated with them.

For this exercise the room should be well-lit, with a large mirror, preferably full-length. First, take off all of your clothes and stand and gaze at each other for a minute. Stand about three feet apart and look into each other's eyes. Slowly take in your partner's facial features—notice things that you have never noticed before or things that you haven't taken the time to notice in a while.

Now both partners should lower their gaze to take in the chest area. Think of this as a sensate focus caress using the eyes instead of the hands. Let your eyes move slowly over your partner's body, as if you were caressing him or her; take your time and gaze at each body part for as long as it takes to visually enjoy it. Mutually shift your gaze downward over the chest, abdomen, and legs. Take time to look at each other's genitals. Each partner should then turn around so that the other person can look at the back side of the body.

Your experience of this part of the body image exercise will probably be different from my experience of the exercise with clients. When I do this exercise with clients, it is the first time that we have seen each other nude. You may have seen your partner's body naked many times. If that is the case, use the first part of the exercise (looking at each other) to appreciate, rather than to see for the first time.

Even if you have seen each other nude many times, it may not have been acceptable in your relationship to stare at certain body parts, such as the breasts or genitals. Or you may be in the habit of wearing sleepwear to bed, and sexual activity may take place only with the lights off. Partners may not be in the habit of walking around the house nude due to the presence of other family members. For whatever reason, you may not have much experience seeing your partner nude or being seen in the nude, so nudity in itself may cause anxiety. If you feel anxious or self-conscious during this part of the exercise, take some deep breaths and express the fact that you feel anxiety to your partner.

There may be other sources of anxiety during this part of the exercise. Men and women usually have different anxieties about their bodies and about being nude in front of a partner.

For men, there are two beliefs that may cause anxiety in this situation. The first is the feeling that one's penis is too small. *Every* male client I have worked with has expressed the belief during this exercise that his penis was not large enough!

A second source of anxiety for men during this exercise is whether they will have an erection or not. Men have different ideas about how long it *should* take them to get an erection when they are naked with a woman. Some expect to have an erection immediately; others may allow themselves one minute or five minutes. Others think that they should not have an erection at all and are embarrassed if they do have one.

The body image exercise is not a sexual exercise. Try to determine what your "time frame" is for having an erection, and take the pressure off yourself. If you do have an erection during the exercise, just enjoy it and keep doing the exercise. Don't try to make your erection harder, and don't try to make it go away. It is perfectly normal to either have or not have an erection during this exercise.

While men's anxieties tend to be about their genitals, women tend to worry about being overweight, and about whether their partner will find some of their body parts unacceptable. Most women tend to think that their breasts are too small or too saggy, and that their hips and thighs are too wide. Part of their reason for feeling overweight is that our culture and society place a totally unwarranted emphasis on thinness, idealizing a body that is quite honestly unattainable for the vast majority of women. Hopefully, doing this exercise and the ones that follow will help you to accept your body more.

If you do feel anxious about whether your partner finds your body attractive, just accept the fact that you have these feelings for now. Doing the body image exercise and the other activities that follow does not require a body that meets certain standards of attractiveness.

Your anxieties and feelings about your body and about your partner's reaction to it are real. The body image exercise will help you learn to accept negative feelings about your body and learn to not let these feelings get in the way of your enjoyment. You will also learn how your partner feels about his or her body. I hope that the outcome of this exercise is that you develop the attitude, "While there may be certain aspects of my body that I am not ecstatic about, my body is capable of feeling good. I can have sensual and sexual enjoyment of my body if I accept myself the way I am."

❤

In the next part of the body image exercise, one partner is passive and one is active. Let's say that the woman decides to be active first. She should take a long look at herself in the mirror and describe all the parts of her body, and her feelings associated with these parts. The man will sit comfortably and watch and listen.

While you are listening, you may find that you disagree with your partner's description or feelings about certain body parts. As the passive person, you should not interrupt, make comments, or ask questions. You will have an opportunity for feedback when you are both through with the exercise. Try not to negate the other person's feelings—just accept that he or she feels that way.

When you are active, look at yourself in the mirror carefully. Use a hand mirror to examine the back of your body. Starting with your hair, tell your partner whether you like or dislike it, what you like or dislike about it, any good or bad feelings or memories that are associated with it, whether you like to touch it or have it touched, and how it feels.

Do the same for all your other body parts. Here is a list so you don't leave anything out: hair, eyes, ears, nose, mouth, face, neck, shoulders, back, breasts/chest, arms, hands, stomach, waist, hips, thighs, buttocks, genitals, legs, feet. Also include height, weight, body hair, and any characteristics such as moles, birthmarks, or scars.

After you have described your body parts and told your partner how you feel about them, examine your body as a whole. Tell your partner what your favorite and least favorite parts are—what do you consider your best and worst features? What parts cause you anxiety? Which parts do you like to have touched or looked at? Which parts don't you like to have touched or looked at, and why? What would you change if you could change anything about your body? What would *you* like to look like, and why?

After you have switched roles and the other partner has described his or her body, discuss the following: Did you feel your partner was realistic about his or her body? Why or why not? Which parts of your partner's body do you especially like? Believe your partner's feelings about your body, even though they may not coincide with yours.

Please remember that this is not a time for bringing up any negative or critical feelings about your partner, or about your past or current relationship. It is a time to learn how you and your partner feel about your own bodies in preparation for learning to touch each other in a new way.

❤

This is not an easy exercise to do because we don't usually discuss our feelings about our body with other people. However, it will accomplish several things. It will build trust between you and your partner. It provides practice in communicating about feelings. It provides information about how your partner feels about his or her body. This can be important, because a poor body image can cause people to shy away from sexual activities. Also, people may have certain body parts that they are sensitive about.

Getting your feelings and anxieties about your body out in the open can eliminate further negative experiences. You may also learn that your partner's reaction to being touched may have much less to do with the way you touch than with his or her own anxieties about body image.

> A client of mine, *Alex*, did not like to kiss, and this was causing a problem for him in relationships. In the body image exercise he revealed that he had been in an accident and broken his jaw when he was a teenager and had to have major reconstructive surgery on his face and especially his lips. The scars from the surgery were no longer visible, but the trauma stayed with him, and made him self-conscious. He had never told a sexual partner that kissing created anxieties for him or why. The women he had been with had not known why he refused to kiss, and thought that it was a problem with them, which made *them* anxious.

It is possible that either your partner or you has had a traumatic experience in the past that has caused you to feel uncomfortable about your naked body, or embarrassed about a certain body part. For example, a woman may have a sense of discomfort on a deeper level because of a molestation episode in her past that she had previously kept secret. She may decide to tell her partner about this during the body image process, and feels a great sense of risk in doing so. If the body image exercise does bring up a powerful memory or issue for you, remember that sometimes just getting it out in the open can help to release it, although you will probably need the assistance of a qualified therapist to deal with the issue completely. If a painful memory comes up for your partner, accept his or her feelings completely and be very supportive.

I have rarely encountered a client who had a severe body image problem, but I realize that it may be easier for a client and me to do the exercise because the client expects me to be supportive.

❤

Another purpose of the body image exercise is to find out if you and your partner have *realistic* views of your bodies. As a woman, you may find your body unattractive and think your partner is not telling the truth when he says that he likes your breasts or your thighs. If you are a man, you may feel that your penis is too small, when in fact your partner may like the way your penis looks and feels. These feelings about yourself and the way you look are probably not negative enough to stand in the way of doing sensate focus exercises together. Problems arise when a person's body image is either totally unrealistic or so negative that he or she cannot relax enough to enjoy sensual arousal.

An example of a client with an unrealistic body image would be a person who is actually fairly good-looking, but whose self-esteem is so low that she thinks she is ugly. I use a female example because this unrealistic body image is more characteristic of female clients. Another example would be a man who has completely let himself go, to the point of neglecting personal hygiene, yet thinks he is good-looking and appealing to women. Neither of these people is realistic about looks, but this is only a problem if it interferes with doing the sensate focus exercises.

When I do the body image exercise with clients, I find that most male clients have a positive attitude toward their bodies in general. Women are much more likely to pick themselves apart for not living up to a cultural ideal of attractiveness.

I have worked with clients of all levels of attractiveness. I have never worked with a client who was so unattractive that it interfered with our ability to do the exercises. Both attractive and unattractive bodies feel good to touch. At the skin-to-skin level, it really only matters what the body feels like, not what it looks like. Looks have no bearing on "sensuality," which has to do with touching and feeling rather than visual stimulation.

There is no research that I know of on whether attractive people have more satisfying sex lives than less attractive people. However, it is possible that there is some aspect of your appearance that you would like to change. There are a number of excellent books available on skin care, health, exercise, and clothing choice. You are an adult, and you have a large degree of choice about how you look. While appearance may be given too much importance in this culture, making yourself more attractive *can* boost your self-esteem, and that is always worthwhile.

Back Caress

So far in this program you have done spoon breathing, the face caress, and the body image exercise. Spoon breathing is done to give you a chance to relax and make the transition from the everyday stresses of your life to a mode where you will be receptive to sensual arousal. During the face caress, you learned to focus on touch and you practiced being in active and passive roles. In the body image process, you and your partner communicated feelings about your bodies, perhaps for the first time.

The back caress will introduce several new elements. It is the first sensate focus exercise that you will do in the nude. It is the first sensate focus exercise which will involve parts of the body that you may already associate with sexual arousal, for example, the buttocks.

To do the back caress, you need a bed or some other comfortable surface with plenty of room for both of you to stretch out. As always, you need a quiet room where you will not be disturbed. You may also want to use a large towel and some talcum powder.

Before beginning the back caress, please review the basic principles for doing all of the sensate focus exercises, "The Sensual Mindset," in Appendix I.

The back caress is done in the nude, and includes the entire back of the body from the neck to the feet, but not the genitals. Do some spoon breathing for about five minutes to relax. Decide which partner will be active first. The passive partner should lie comfortably, face down, with a towel underneath. The passive partner may keep the arms at his or her sides or underneath the head. The active partner should lie next to the passive partner and maintain as much body contact as possible during the exercise.

Remember—focus, breathe, relax.

The active person begins to stroke the passive person's back with one hand. Begin at the neck. Slowly run your palm or your fingers over the shoulder blades and then down the spine. Remember, this is not a massage.

The object is to use your hand to feel as good as you possibly can by touching the back of your partner's body.

The way that I usually do the back caress is to snuggle up against my partner and use my hand to reach as many parts of the back as I can. Then I change positions so that I can touch the legs and feet. I usually use some type of baby powder or body powder to do this caress. It increases the sensual arousal for me because my hands tend to perspire, which makes my touch a little rough. You may decide for yourself whether you think powder would feel good.

Some books recommend doing this caress with the active person straddling the partner's back and using both hands. I find that I get much more feeling when I do the caress as I have described—lying next to the person and with a minimum of effort. I find that doing a back caress in a traditional massage position (straddling the partner) tends to set the exercise up as a performance situation right at the beginning, and then the expectation is conveyed to my partner that he must respond. Also, if you do the caress as I suggest, you will be much more comfortable and you won't have sore leg muscles from sitting or kneeling. This leaves you free to have more sensual arousal during the exercise.

When you are the active partner, caress your partner's back, buttocks, and legs for your own pleasure. Think of your partner's body as a playground and touch anything that feels good to you.

You will maximize your ability to focus on sensations if you close your eyes during the caress. Remember to stroke your partner *slowly.* If you have trouble focusing, consciously slow your caressing motion down to half the speed it was before. If thoughts about whether your partner is enjoying the exercise intrude, bring your mind back to the exact point of contact between your skin and your partner's skin.

Pay attention to how the different body parts feel when you slowly stroke them with your palm, versus your fingertips. Some areas on the back of the body that may feel especially good to touch include the back of the neck, the spine, and the thighs right underneath the buttocks. You may find that different parts of your partner's back feel especially good to you.

As a variation you could use your upper body to caress, in addition to just your hand. Use your hair, face, or chest to caress if you can do it for your own enjoyment and not worry about whether your partner likes it.

Pay attention to texture and temperature. Run your fingers around the depression at the base of your partner's spine. Run the tip of one finger slowly up your partner's backbone. You may want to conclude the caress with a final gesture, like a soft pinch on the earlobe or by running your fingers through your partner's hair.

If you are doing the back caress and you feel or see your partner's body tensing (for example, as you touch the thighs, you see the muscles tighten), lightly pinch or press down on the thigh as a signal to your partner to relax. You should be able to notice any tightening or moving around. Remind your partner to breathe, and continue with the caress.

When you are passive in the back caress, enjoy yourself. Soak up the sensations like a sponge. Breathe evenly and relax your muscles. Keep your mind on the exact point of contact where your partner is touching you. Try not to move; just passively accept stimulation into your body. The only time you need to communicate with your partner is if he or she does something that bothers you.

If you become sexually aroused during the back caress, fine. Just enjoy the arousal and bring your mind back to the exact point of contact. We are not concerned with sexual arousal yet. What we are doing is practicing the sensate focus technique so that it becomes a natural action whenever you touch your partner or whenever you are touched. We are building a foundation so that when you move on to exercises that are more overtly sexual, you will naturally focus on how your body feels when you touch or are touched.

Each partner should do the back caress for about twenty minutes. Please observe the active and passive distinctions—there should be no mutual caressing at this stage.

❤

The most common problem in doing the back caress is using a massage technique rather than caressing. The goal is not to manipulate the muscles under the skin in order to make the person being massaged feel good. The idea is rather for *your* skin to become alive with sensations. You should not even be aware of muscles—you should just be aware of skin.

A more serious problem is failure to stay within the limits of the exercise. For example, did either partner reach between the legs and attempt to include the genitals in the caress? The genitals are not part of the back caress, and when you include parts of the body that are not in the exercise, you put performance demands on your partner and interfere with the ability of both of you to focus on sensations, to enjoy the caress, and to learn from the caress. If you touch the genitals during the back caress, you are jumping ahead to a future exercise, which means you aren't in the here and now. You need to learn the basics of sensate focus first.

If you go beyond the limits of an exercise, your partner will go into a vigilant, "spectatoring" mode, instead of being able to enjoy and focus, and will wonder "Will he keep doing this? Should I say something?" This vigilant response is physiologically incompatible with the relaxation that is necessary to enjoy sensate focus exercises.

Underlying this problem of jumping ahead is feeling sexually aroused and feeling that you have to do something about it. If you do experience arousal during the caress, just enjoy it. As the passive partner, you should not wiggle around or push yourself against your partner's hand or the bed. Men, if you get so aroused during the caress that you get an erection or even ejaculate, just enjoy it. Don't try to push the arousal away or make it better somehow. Women, if you lubricate or feel aroused, just enjoy it and continue the exercise. Contrary to popular belief, nothing bad will happen to you if you become aroused but don't have an orgasm. You don't need to experience sexual arousal in order to learn from the caress, but if it happens, you can still complete the exercise.

Another problem you may encounter in doing the back caress may be that anxiety is still present. Your partner will notice if you are tensing muscles in your thighs or buttocks during the exercise. Other signs of anxiety include rapid breathing that does not slow down or squirming and twitching during the caress. What can you do to get rid of the anxiety?

If you are active and notice your partner tensing, moving, or breathing rapidly after the exercise has gone on for a few minutes, stop the caress and talk quietly to your partner about this. If your partner is feeling some anxiety, go back to the spoon breathing for a few minutes, or do some deep breathing of the kind you learned in the self-exercises.

To review—did you have a problem with being anxious? If so, you need to focus on your breathing. Did you have a problem remaining passive? If so, you need to relax your muscles. Did you try to please your partner? Did you have a problem staying in the here and now?

Were you trying to do a good job? You need to practice focusing on the touch. Did you become distracted? You need to practice a slower touch. Remember—focus, breathe, and *relax.*

❤

In these initial sensate focus exercises like the back caress, people with specific sexual concerns may find it hard not to be preoccupied with their issues. For example, if you are having erection problems, your biggest concern may be whether you are getting an erection or not. Remember, we are not concerned with erections yet and it is not necessary to have an erection during the back caress. If your problem is premature ejaculation, you may be worried that you will ejaculate during this exercise. If you feel any sexual charge at all during the exercise, don't try to make it better and don't try to push it away. Just accept it. It's all right if you ejaculate during this exercise as long as you don't try to stop it. If your problem is inhibited ejaculation, you may be tempted to go beyond the limits of the exercise to something more sexual. Keep the exercise separate from any sexual activity that you might do later.

If you are a woman and your problem is the inability to have an orgasm, your biggest concern during the back caress will probably be whether you are aroused. Don't try to make the exercise any better, but if you do feel any arousal, don't try to push it away. Remain passive when in the passive role, and when you are active, don't try to turn yourself on—just enjoy the touch.

If you have vaginismus or a phobia about sexual activity, anxiety may be your biggest concern here. Your partner can monitor your anxiety and help you make sure that you are breathing evenly and that your muscles are relaxed.

♥

In this session, you have already talked with your partner after the body image process. After the back caress, here are some things you should discuss.

What part of the time were you able to focus when you were active? When you were passive? If you had a problem staying focused, what type of thoughts distracted you?

Which role was more enjoyable for you, active or passive? Why? Were you able to remain passive when in the passive role?

Were you able to do the caress for your own pleasure, or were you trying to please your partner at any point? Did you feel pressured to perform or respond?

Did you feel more or less anxious as the caress went on? Were you able to relax and enjoy the caress? Did you notice anxiety in your partner's body?

Did you feel any sexual arousal during any part of the caress?

Were you able to stay within the bounds of the exercise?

It may be helpful at this point to use a scale of "1" to "10" to explore some of your reactions (as you learned to do in the exercises you did alone). A "1" would be "no anxiety" and a "10" would be "high anxiety." How anxious, on a scale from "1" to "10," did you feel when you started the caress? When you finished the caress? How much sexual arousal did you feel? If you did not feel any, that is fine. The back caress is sensual, not sexual, but if you did feel arousal, acknowledge it.

Sequence for Session 2
Body image — First person — 15 minutes
Body image — Second person — 15 minutes
Feedback

Spoon breathing — 5 minutes
Back caress — First person — 20 minutes
Spoon breathing — 5 minutes
Back caress — Second person — 20 minutes
Spoon breathing — 5 minutes
Feedback

Chapter 8

---------- ❤ ----------

Session 3: Front Caress
Session 4: Genital Caress
Session 5: Oral Sex

Session 3: Front Caress

The next session is the front caress with casual genital
touching. You will need to set aside an hour to an hour
and a half for this session. You will need a quiet room,
talcum powder, and a towel.

Before you do the front caress, do a few minutes of
spoon breathing to relax. Then each partner can do a
focusing caress to become even more relaxed. A focusing
caress is a short version of a nonsexual caress done to
make a transition into a new, more sexual exercise. The
focusing caress may be either the face caress or the back
caress. You may decide which you would like to do. You
should each do a focusing caress for ten minutes prior
to starting the front caress.

The passive partner should lie on his or her back in a relaxed position. The front caress includes the whole front of the body from the head to the feet. It also includes the genitals, but only in a "casual" way, which means that you do not spend any more time on the genitals than you would do on any other part of the body. The front caress does not include finger penetration of the vagina; it is a sensual exercise and is not done to arouse your partner sexually.

The instructions for the front caress are the same as for the back caress. The active person should lie next to the passive person and maintain as much full body contact as possible. Use some talcum powder on your partner's body and on your hand if you tend to perspire.

The active person should *slowly* stroke the passive person's body, beginning with the face, neck, shoulders and arms, and moving down across the chest, stomach, abdomen and genitals to the thighs, calves, and feet. Caress as slowly and lightly as possible. It is important to be systematic; don't jump from the feet to the head but rather proceed down the body, caressing one part at a time. It is also important to maintain contact with the partner's body. Keep your hand on your partner as much as possible so as to avoid surprising or startling touches. You can help your partner to relax by maintaining contact on the body with your hand.

Touch for your own pleasure. Think of your partner's body as a playground and touch whatever parts feel good, in the way that feels best for you. You may use your palm, fingers, back of the hand, or arm. Toward the end of the caress you may want to kneel and caress your partner's body with your face, hair, or chest. This can be very sensuous. Don't concern yourself with what your partner is thinking or feeling during the caress. Your partner will tell you if you do something that makes him or her uncomfortable.

Your partner will feel pressured to respond if you caress too rapidly or too roughly. Avoid putting pressure on your partner and maximize your own enjoyment by caressing as slowly and gently as you can. Focus on the exact point of contact between your skin and your partner's skin. If your mind wanders to other things, bring it back to the exact point of contact. If you do the caress for your own enjoyment and focus as much as you can, your partner will enjoy the caress also.

When you are passive, your only task is to relax and enjoy the caress. Focus on the exact point of contact. The only time you need to say anything to your partner is if he or she does anything that bothers you. Otherwise, try to relax and breathe while remaining receptive and still. If you feel yourself tensing, slow your breathing down and sink your leg muscles into the bed.

If you are in the active role, you may notice that your partner is not relaxing. Some signs that your partner is anxious (besides muscle tension) include rapid breathing, fast heartbeat, and a quivering stomach. If you can see that your partner's body is tense, lightly pinch or press on the body part that is tense as a signal to your partner to relax. Your partner may not even be aware that he or she is tense.

The front caress has the potential to be more anxiety-producing than the back caress. When we lie on our backs, our chests and genitals are exposed and we feel vulnerable. One thing you can do to promote relaxation is to slow your touch down. Another is to slowly stroke the abdominal area with circular strokes. You are not trying to "fix" your partner. Your major concern should be touching in a way that feels good for you. Take a few deep breaths yourself—your partner will probably imitate your breathing. If the front caress becomes too anxiety-producing, back up to an earlier exercise, or simply to a body part which is less threatening to touch, such as the face, until breathing has slowed.

Because the front caress has the potential to be more sexual, there will be more temptation to slip back into your old habits of touching. You may find yourself trying to turn your partner on. This will make it harder for your partner to stay in the here and now because he or she may think, "I wonder if he will touch my genitals again?" or, "Oh no, she's heading down toward my penis."

It may also be more difficult to remain passive than it was in previous exercises because you may be used to moving or moaning when your breasts or genitals are touched. Allow yourself to *experience* the arousal, without trying to do anything about it. If you feel aroused, don't try to make it better by moving around, and don't try to push it away. By remaining passive you are teaching your body how to feel as much arousal as it can possibly feel. If you move around at this stage, you will lower your arousal rather than make it stronger.

❤

If you are a woman who is having orgasm problems, it may be difficult for you to remain passive during this exercise. When active, you may be tempted to arouse yourself by rubbing against your partner. You also may be tempted to try to please your partner. You have the potential during the front caress to learn how much enjoyment you can get from touching your partner in a sensual way. You also have the potential to learn to relax and allow your body to experience maximum stimulation. The front caress can also give you practice in learning to leave yourself alone and respond the way *your body* wants to, rather than the way you think your partner wants you to.

If you have vaginismus, or are experiencing general

sexual anxiety, the front caress is a very important exercise for you, and you may have to repeat it several times in order to learn to relax fully. You may feel severe anxiety and muscle tightening as your partner's hand approaches your genitals. At all times keep your attention on where your partner is touching, rather than looking ahead to where he may touch next. Your partner can help you by giving you a gentle touch if your muscles are tensing, if you seem to be unaware of it.

If you are having erection problems, the front caress is a crucial exercise for you. It may bring out all the fears you have about not getting an erection. Do not *expect* the front caress to give you an erection. It probably will not. If it does, just allow it to happen. Do not move around and do not squeeze your PC muscle, as this will diminish your arousal. If you have an erection, you may feel you want to use it. Instead, see this as your first chance to practice relaxing with an erection, rather than doing something with it.

If you are concerned about premature ejaculation, you may be worried that you will become too aroused and ejaculate. That's fine. If you ejaculate during the caress, don't worry about it. Let your partner know, so it is not a surprise. Relax as much as you can and allow your body to experience the ejaculation. The important thing is not how long you last, but whether you can leave yourself alone and allow your body to experience arousal. At this stage, it is important for you to learn to relax your body as much as possible, and your partner can help you to recognize when your body is showing signs of anxiety.

If you are having problems with inhibited ejaculation, it may be difficult for you to leave yourself alone and proceed slowly in this exercise. Be especially attuned to whether you may be subtly pressuring your partner through your touch.

There are a number of ways that you can do the front caress, depending on what your problem is and how you feel. If you are very relaxed, use your face, hair, or chest to caress your partner. If you are highly anxious, it may be best to do only part of the front caress; for example, you may want to start with just the top half of the body. Or, you may want to do the front of the body without touching the genitals.

If you are very, *very* anxious, you may want to do a preliminary exercise in which you take your partner's hand and guide it over your body. You may do any of these variations, as long as you discuss it with your partner first and agree on exactly what to do ahead of time. Being able to successfully predict your partner's touch will do wonders in helping you to trust and relax.

❤

After the exercise, do spoon breathing and then discuss the same questions you went through after the back caress.

How is your ability to focus when you are active and when you are passive? Have you noticed an improvement in focusing over the sessions? Since you have done several exercises now, you have some experiences that you can compare. Was it easier to focus during the face caress, back caress, or front caress? Does the fact that the front caress is more sexual make it more difficult for you to stay focused? Ideally, you should be fairly good at focusing on the touch by now.

Were you able to relax when you were passive? Were you able to lie still and let your body experience sensual arousal, or did you feel the urge to move around?

When active, were you able to do the exercise for your own pleasure? Are you getting a sense of when you are pleasing yourself and when you lapse into wondering how your partner feels? Did you enjoy yourself?

Did you feel as if your partner was pressuring you to respond at any time? Did you worry about whether you were becoming sexually aroused? Did you bring yourself back to the touch and just leave yourself alone?

How was your anxiety level? Are you becoming less anxious with each session, or more anxious? How is your anxiety level on a scale of "1" to "10"?

Did you feel any sexual arousal during the front caress? If you did, fine; if not, fine. Give it a number on the "1" to "10" scale and forget about it for now. Remember, we are still building a foundation of relaxation and sensuality, and we are not concerned about sexual arousal yet.

Did you want to go beyond the exercise to something more sexual? Were you able to stay with the limits of the exercise?

Sequence for Session 3
Spoon breathing — 5 minutes
Focusing caress — First person (back or face)
— 10 minutes
Focusing caress — Second person (back or face)
— 10 minutes
Spoon breathing — 5 minutes
Front caress — First person — 20 minutes
Front caress — Second person — 20 minutes
Spoon breathing — 5 minutes
Feedback

Session 4: Genital Caress

Your first genital caress session will take about one hour to an hour and a half. You will need a quiet room, a towel, some talcum powder, and some kind of lubricant that both partners like. Some suggestions are K-Y Jelly, mineral oil, baby oil, or massage oil. I tend to use an oil-base product rather than a water-base product because oils seem to warm up more rapidly on the body.

Begin your genital caress session with some spoon breathing. Then each partner may choose a focusing caress (either a back caress or a face caress). Don't slack off or become mechanical about these initial caresses— do them for at least ten minutes each, and pay attention to what you are feeling.

Begin by caressing the front of your partner's body with powder as you did in the front caress session. This time you will spend at least half the caress on the genitals. After about ten minutes of the front caress, wipe the powder off your hand and warm up some baby oil in your hand. Slowly begin to caress your partner's genitals with your fingers.

If your passive partner is a woman, use lots of lubrication and *slowly* move your fingers over your partner's outer vaginal lips, inner vaginal lips, perineum, and clitoris. Then *slowly* insert your finger inside the vagina. Pay attention to how the different lips feel and how the different parts feel inside the vagina. Feel the vaginal walls and the muscles around the vaginal opening. Think of the inside of the vagina as a clock and move your fingers from twelve o'clock all the way around in a circle.

The genital caress is the same as the other caresses in that you are touching for your own pleasure. If you slip into rubbing your partner's clitoris or trying to turn her on in some way, she will be able to feel this shift in your intention. She has agreed to be passive and to not respond no matter what you do, so stay with the exercise. Take this opportunity to really learn how your partner's genitals feel without any interference or distractions.

As part of this caress, lie between your partner's legs as you are caressing and learn what her genitals look like as well. Many sexual problems are caused by ignorance about the partner's genitals. Take this opportunity to learn every hair and every fold of skin. If you feel yourself becoming mechanical or bored with the caress, slow down. Caress the genitals for ten to fifteen minutes. Do it for yourself. If you can see your partner's body tensing, lightly pat her legs as a signal to relax.

If your passive partner is a man, caress the front of your partner's body for about ten minutes and then warm some lubricant in your hand. Slowly caress the penis and scrotum with your fingers. Don't try to turn your partner on. Do the caress so it feels as good for you as possible. If you slip into wishing your partner would get an erection, bring yourself back to your enjoyment of the caress. Your partner has agreed not to move around or respond verbally, so take this opportunity to learn what your partner's genitals feel and look like. Slowly move your fingers around the shaft and head of the penis, then slowly run your fingers around each testicle.

It doesn't matter whether your partner has an erection during the genital caress. A soft penis feels just as good to the touch as an erect one—the sensations are not better or worse, just different. Experience exactly what the skin feels like on the different areas of the genitals. If you see your partner's body becoming tense, signal him to relax with a light tap on the leg. Make sure your partner is not holding his breath. If he becomes aroused and ejaculates, gently wipe him off and continue the caress. Do the genital caress for ten to fifteen minutes.

When you are passive, lie on your back with your legs slightly spread. Place your arms at your sides or under your head. Close your eyes. As you receive the genital caress, all you need to do is focus, breathe, and relax. The only time you need to talk to your partner is if he or she does something that hurts you. Allow yourself to soak up all the sensations like a sponge.

It may be difficult to remain passive, but remember—if you try to make your arousal better by moving, you are in fact working against yourself by diminishing your arousal. Also, be sure not to flex your PC muscle during this exercise. If you become aroused, that's fine. If you don't, that's fine, too. If you get an erection, or have an orgasm, fine. What matters is whether you can leave yourself alone and enjoy yourself. Don't force anything. Just passively experience the feelings— and enjoy them!

❤

The biggest barriers to the genital caress are anxiety and performance pressure. Focusing should not be a problem—by now you should be able to focus, as long as you reduce your anxiety and get rid of performance pressure.

Anxiety will manifest itself in the body. Is your breathing irregular or are your muscles tensing? Your partner can help you recognize and correct this. Performance pressure will manifest itself in distracting thoughts such as, "I wonder if I'm starting to get hard," or, "I wonder if I'm going to have an orgasm." If you catch yourself thinking instead of feeling, bring your mind back to the touch.

Your partner will probably be able to tell if you are having distracting thoughts just by watching your body. If you are focusing on your genitals, blood will flow to that area and the genitals will warm up, whereas if you are spectatoring, blood will flow away from the genital area.

If you have a problem with vaginismus, the genital caress is a very important exercise for you. Hopefully you learned to relax while your partner touched your pubic hair during the front caress. You may have needed to guide your partner's hand. That is fine. You may have needed to proceed slowly and do the front caress several times, which is also fine. If you are able to relax with the help of your partner's feedback, you can do the genital caress.

You may also need to do the genital caress several times. The first time you do it, try it as described and see how you feel. Your partner may coach you in breathing and relaxing while slowly and gently caressing your vaginal lips in a nondemand fashion. The most important thing for you is to focus on the relaxation of your stomach, leg, and buttocks muscles.

The first time your partner is able to insert a finger, he or she should just leave it there without moving, while you continue to breathe and relax your muscles. The important thing is for your partner to move slowly. Focus on your partner's finger inside your vagina.

If the full genital caress causes anxiety for you, you may want to break it into a series of smaller steps, such as touching the lips, putting the tip of the finger inside, putting all of the finger inside, and moving the finger inside. Or you may need to try each new step and then back up to a more comfortable exercise a number of times.

It is all right to use the basic description of the genital caress as a blueprint for designing your own program to work with the specific fears that you have or the specific levels of anxiety you experience.

You may also want to do a version of the genital caress in which you and your partner give each other feedback about what types of touching you enjoy on your genitals. Do the caress as described. Then, at the end of the caress, you as the passive partner should describe one or two things which your partner did that you especially liked. Then ask your partner to do them again. Allow yourself to enjoy this touch for several minutes. If it is not exactly what you wanted, give your partner more feedback, until he or she does the caress exactly as before.

Then tell your partner something that he or she didn't do, but that you would like. You may take your partner's hand and gently guide it to receive what you want for a few minutes. This aspect of the genital caress will help you and your partner learn to communicate with each other about what you like in a nonthreatening way.

❤

After the genital caress, you and your partner should give feedback to each other as you did after the back and front caresses. As usual, the important questions are: How was your concentration? Which role was more comfortable for you? Were you pressuring yourself to respond? Did you feel your partner pressuring you to respond? Were you able to remain passive and let the sensations in? Were you able to do the caress for your own pleasure? Were you able to follow the instructions? How was your anxiety level on a scale from "1" to "10"? Did you experience any sexual arousal during the caress? If you did, that's fine; if not, that's fine also.

Sequence for Session 4
Spoon breathing — 5 minutes
Focusing caress — First person (back or face)
— 10 minutes
Focusing caress — Second person (back or face)
— 10 minutes
Spoon breathing — 5 minutes
Genital caress — First person — 15 minutes
Genital caress — Second person — 15 minutes
Spoon breathing — 5 minutes
Feedback

Session 5: Oral Sex

After you have done the genital caress often enough to become comfortable with it, you are ready to try oral sex. Oral sex is another variation on the genital caress. Before I describe the exercise, let me say a few words about oral sex in general.

Many couples have either never experienced oral sex or find the practice negative or even revolting. For that matter, many people "perform" oral sex but either don't enjoy it, feel coerced into it, or just do it to please the other person and get it over with. Oral sex is a sexual practice that is probably associated with more performance anxiety than any other practice, possibly even more than intercourse.

Many sexual self-help books talk about oral sex as though there are techniques that will guarantee orgasm in the sexual partner, or techniques that every man or every woman will enjoy all of the time. This is misleading. Being able to enjoy oral sex depends more on how relaxed and focused you are than it does on what techniques you use.

If you recognize that you have a negative attitude toward oral sex, relax. There is nothing that is inherently dirty about genitals. If your partner has washed his or her genitals and is free of infection, there is nothing to worry about. In fact, most people's genitals are cleaner than their mouths.

I encourage you to experience oral sex in the context of a sensate focus exercise because there are few things as enjoyable as doing or receiving a sensuous, nondemand, oral genital caress. Your tongue is an organ with a lot of nerve endings—why deny yourself the pleasure you could receive by using it? You may be surprised to find that, when the performance aspect is removed from oral sex, you will like it. What if it does smell funny or taste funny? Humans acclimate rather rapidly to odors; that is, after a few seconds we find that we don't notice them. Also, if you lick with certain parts of your tongue you will find that you are able to taste, whereas if you lick with other parts, such as the tip, you do not taste. Allow yourself to discover which parts of your tongue are more sensitive and enjoyable.

Don't expect to enjoy oral sex right away if you have little experience with it; it will take some time. But the best way to learn to enjoy oral sex is to do it often, in a nondemand way.

If you are afraid that the genitals will not smell good, ask your partner to shower or wash before the exercise. In fact, it might be a good idea to shower together and wash each other's genitals, or wash them as part of the exercise.

Think of sensate focus oral sex with your partner as simply using your tongue instead of your hand to do a genital caress. The same instructions apply and, if you have been doing the sensate focus exercises and learning from them, you are probably already anticipating what I am going to say next.

Do the caress for your own pleasure.

Do it with a person who remains totally passive.

Do it slowly and to explore.

When you are active, do not pressure your partner to respond.

Do the caress in a sensuous manner, to make your tongue feel good rather than to turn your partner on.

Begin with a front caress for five minutes or so. Then caress the genitals with your hand as you did during the genital caress.

To begin the oral genital caress, if the passive partner is a woman, be sure both of you are in comfortable positions. She should either lie down with your face between her legs or sit leaning back with her legs spread apart.

Then, *slowly* move your tongue along the inner thighs, outer lips, inner lips, clitoral hood, and in and out of the vagina. Do this for ten or fifteen minutes. You may want to use your lips also. Focus on the exact point of contact, and explore how the different parts of your partner's genitals feel and taste on the different parts of your mouth.

If your tongue, chin, or neck starts to get tired or sore, change positions and relax. You may be holding your tongue too stiffly in an effort to please your partner. Your tongue should be relaxed.

Do not stiffen your tongue and rub it forcefully against the clitoris. Do not forcefully suck or slurp at the inner or outer lips. Do not insert a finger into the vagina or rub the clitoris with your finger while you lick the vagina. Your partner will be likely to interpret any of these actions as a demand to respond and she will remain anxious and not be able to relax. The point of the exercise is for you to enjoy sensations in your mouth and for your partner to be able to enjoy herself with no demands on her to show how much she likes it.

If your passive partner is a man, spend about five minutes on a front caress. Then caress your partner's genitals with your hand for a few minutes until you are focused and you are both relaxed.

Then *slowly* use your tongue and lips to lick all over his penis and scrotum and thighs. You may want to slowly take the whole penis in your mouth and slowly let it back out again. Explore freely, and do what makes your tongue feel good. Lick the area behind the testicles. Insert your tongue into the creases between the thighs and scrotum. Experience how each different area feels or tastes on your lips and tongue.

Do not suck on the penis in such a way that your head moves up and down. Only your tongue and lips should move during this exercise. If your neck or tongue becomes tired or sore, move to a different position. Your tongue should remain relaxed and not stiff. If you feel pressured to perform, stop and caress some other part of your partner's body until you feel that you are focused enough to enjoy the oral sex again. It is best if you respond to what *you* want, rather than what you think your partner wants. If your partner indicates that he is about to ejaculate, decide whether to take the semen in your mouth or whether to temporarily stop the caress while your partner ejaculates. If you have not done the caress for the full fifteen minutes, wipe off the semen and continue the caress.

Do not use your hand to masturbate your partner during this caress. Remember, you are doing this caress only for your own pleasure. It doesn't matter whether your partner gets aroused or not or whether he ejaculates or not. What does matter is that you do what feels good for you and that you focus on the feelings in your mouth during the caress.

❤

After the oral genital caress, you and your partner will give each other feedback about your ability to focus, feelings of performance pressure, and levels of anxiety. Use the feedback session to try to pinpoint any problem areas. For example, if you still feel pressured to respond when your partner licks your genitals, repeat the exercise later and tell your partner during the exercise when you are feeling pressured. Sharing these feelings with your partner during the exercise will bring them out in the open and defuse them. Repeat the oral sex exercise until you are completely able to focus, relax, and enjoy yourself without feeling pressure to perform or respond.

If you have never had oral sex before, it may take you a while to become comfortable with it. Don't expect to be able to focus on it completely immediately. Remember—learning to become comfortable with any new sexual experience takes practice, and enjoyment happens only after comfort has been attained.

Sequence for Session 5
Spoon breathing — 5 minutes
Focusing caress — First person (back or face)
— 10 minutes
Focusing caress — Second person (back or face)
— 10 minutes
Spoon breathing — 5 minutes
Genital caress — oral — First person — 15 minutes
Genital caress — oral — Second person — 15 minutes
Spoon breathing — 5 minutes
Feedback

Sequence for Session 6 (Optional)
Spoon breathing — 5 minutes
Focusing caress — First person — 10 minutes
Focusing caress — Second person — 10 minutes
Spoon breathing — 5 minutes
Genital caress with verbal feedback — First person
— 15 minutes
Genital caress with verbal feedback — Second person
— 15 minutes
Spoon breathing — 5 minutes
Feedback

Chapter 9

♥

Remembering to Play

In this chapter I want to describe some exercises that I learned when I trained as a surrogate partner. I often do them with clients—just to remember that sensuality is *fun*. Try them any time after you complete the basic exercises in the last chapter. Use them to take a break from the program, especially if you feel you are working too hard at trying to get better.

You can do these activities whenever you want a relaxing break from stress. You can do them in any order. You can do them all in one session or one at a time. Use them to reward yourselves now and then for keeping at the other sensate focus exercises in the program.

Foot Caress

The foot caress is a sensate focus exercise sometimes used in sex therapy as a stage between the face caress and the back caress. As I learned to do it, the foot caress includes a foot bath. If you leave out the bath, all you will need is some lotion. If you would like to include the foot bath, you will need two towels, a basin large enough for a person's feet, liquid soap, lotion, and hot water.

Most people like to have their feet touched but are a little embarrassed about it. They think, "What if my feet sweat?" or, "What if they smell funny?" The bath portion of the foot caress should remove these anxieties.

To start, the passive person sits in a chair with his or her feet on the floor. This exercise may be done either clothed or nude, as it includes only the feet and ankles. The active partner fills the basin with warm water and places the passive partner's feet in the water. Add the liquid soap and slowly caress your partner's feet in the water. The foot bath is like any other sensate focus exercise. Touch for your own pleasure, but, believe me, your partner will like this one! Use a light, caressing touch, not massage. Bathe one foot at a time, finding out how the different areas of the foot feel as you bathe them.

When you are done with both feet, lift the feet from the basin one at a time, dry them, and wrap them in separate towels. (You could even have the towels warmed up.) Put aside the basin. Then take one foot from the towel and caress it using the lotion. Again, caress for your own pleasure. Take as long as you like. I usually bathe each foot for about five minutes and then caress each foot for five to ten minutes.

As the passive person during the foot bath and caress, the only thing you need to do is relax and enjoy. Allow yourself to feel pampered. If your partner does something that bothers you, say something, but otherwise concentrate totally on the touch. Relax your feet and just let them hang from your legs. Your partner will lift them into the basin and move them—you don't need to help.

Sensuous Shower

The sensuous shower is a whole-body caress that takes place in the shower. The purpose of the sensuous shower is not to get clean (though you probably will), but to enjoy your own body and your partner's body. There are a number of ways to do the sensuous shower. You can use the system of active and passive roles and take turns, or you can make this exercise a mutual caress, with both partners caressing at the same time.

Include any of the caresses that you have practiced up to this point; for example, you can caress the back, front, and genitals, and you could include oral sex. Use liquid soap and caress any parts of your partner's body that feel good. Caress for your own pleasure when active. When you passive, concentrate on exactly where you are being touched, just as you would during any sensate focus exercise.

If you become aroused during the caress, simply allow yourself to experience the arousal. Don't move on to any activities that you have not yet practiced in the program. Don't try to make your arousal better and don't try to push it away. Just enjoy the feelings of your partner caressing you and the water beating down on your skin. If you have an erection, fine. If you have an orgasm or ejaculation, fine. Don't try to make it happen and don't push it away. After the shower, you may want to dry each other.

The sensuous shower can also be a relaxing prelude to other exercises, such as the genital caress or one of the exercises you will learn in a later chapter.

Tom Jones Dinner

The Tom Jones dinner is named for the sensuous eating scene from the movie. When we did this as part of surrogate training, here is what happened. Everyone in the class (ten to twelve people) brought some type of food that could be eaten with the hands. We spread a sheet on the floor and laid out the foods. We were all naked, and there were three rules: no feeding yourself; no talking; and no utensils. Everybody fed each other. Some of these dinners got pretty wild, with people eating food off each other's bodies. However, the point of the dinner was not to have a wild food orgy, but to learn to enjoy the purely sensuous aspects of eating, free from the restraints of table manners.

You can create the Tom Jones dinner at home for yourself and your partner. First, choose some appropriate foods. Some possibilities are fruit (especially juicy ones such as oranges and peaches), hors d'oeuvres such as cheese and crackers, any meat that can be pulled off a bone, and anything messy that can be licked off fingers and other body parts. In general, anything that is creamy or juicy feels especially good in the mouth. For beverages, use wine or champagne if you drink alcohol, or sparkling water or fruit juice if you do not.

Arrange the food on a sheet to protect your carpeting and furniture. Take off your clothes. Relax, caress each other if you need a transition, then both partners feed each other. Eat with the goal of feeling every sensation as the food passes your lips and through your mouth. Go slowly, just as you would in a caressing exercise. Many of us gobble our food and fail to take the time to enjoy the sensuous aspects of eating. Here is your opportunity.

Watch your partner eat. Put food on your partner's body and slowly lick it off. If you want a drink, your partner can take the drink and then, with a kiss, transfer the liquid to your mouth.

For fun, arrange the foods into the shapes of genitals and other body parts and watch your partner lick and eat them. Finish the Tom Jones dinner by washing each other off with warm wet towels.

Finding the G Spot

The Grafenberg spot, or G spot, is an area inside the vagina. Stimulation of this area, either manually or through intercourse, can be very arousing, but many people are not aware of how to find the G spot.

The G spot is located on the wall of the vagina, the upper wall if the woman is lying on her back. To find it, put some baby oil or other lubricant on your longest finger, usually the middle finger and, turning the hand palm up, insert your finger slowly and gently into the vagina. When the finger is inserted as far as it will go, curl it around as if you were trying to point to the pubic mound from the inside. You will feel a flesh-covered mound that is the pubic bone. At the point behind the pubic bone where your fingertip touches the vaginal wall is the G spot. It will feel a little rougher in texture than the surrounding areas of the vagina. Your partner should be able to tell if you are touching the right place. When her G spot is touched, a woman usually feels as if she has to urinate. Practice caressing the inside of the vagina and then return to the G spot. Include the G spot in future genital caresses if it is comfortable and enjoyable for both of you.

Sexological Exam

When I work with clients, we also include a session called the "sexological exam". This is an examination of the vagina using a speculum, the way a gynecologist does. For most men, and women too, it is a new experience to see what the inside of the vagina looks like. You can see the texture of the vaginal walls and the location of the cervix.

Recently, a client of mine surprised me by bringing in a small dental mirror, the kind that is on a long handle, in order to see the G spot during the sexological exam!

Women, the next time you have a pelvic exam, ask your gynecologist to show you the inside of your vagina with a mirror. Your should be able to obtain a speculum for use with your partner from a woman's health center. Ask them to show you how to use it. Then you can show your partner the inside of the vagina.

Becoming familiar with the location of the G spot and the cervix will benefit you when you and your partner reach the section on exercises for female arousal.

You have now completed the basic sensate focus program. You may want to repeat some of the exercises from Part II that you and your partner especially liked. Feel free to add in the optional, playful sexual exercises mentioned in this chapter whenever you feel you need a change of pace.

Part III

♥

Advanced Exercises

In Part II, we discussed exercises which were designed to help you enhance your sensual awareness and have a more enjoyable sex life. You learned to relax and enjoy your sensuality. Nondemand activities allowed you to focus on your enjoyment while lowering the performance anxiety that too often accompanies intimate sex.

If you were experiencing sexual problems, you may have found that many of the basic sensate focus exercises went a long way toward helping you overcome them. If you are a man who was experiencing erection problems, you may now be having erections through nondemand oral sex with your partner. If you are a woman who was experiencing vaginismus, you may now be relaxed enough to allow finger penetration by your partner. If you were experiencing sexual anxiety or a lack of sexual desire, you may now be able to relax, and you may have more desire for sexual activity.

Remember the "pep talk" I gave you in Part II? I explained sensate focus, nondemand interaction, the here and now, anxiety reduction, and performance pressure. By now these concepts should be ingrained in you. You probably have a good idea of when you are focusing (and when you are not) and when you are anxious (and when you are not). The three instructions I want you to carry over from that section are, "Focus, breathe, relax."

Here is the "pep talk" for Part III: Enjoy yourself! It's easy to get caught up in thoughts such as, "Am I doing this right?" or, "Will I succeed?" You will do just fine if you concentrate on feeling good and having fun together, rather than trying to do things right and trying to get better.

As a result of doing the early sensate focus exercises, your attitude about yourself may have changed. You may now consider yourself a sensuous person. In this section, we will give your body a chance to catch up with your mind.

If you are working on specific sexual problems, please be satisfied with whatever progress you have made. Keep in mind that any noticeable gains in erections, orgasms, or ejaculation control are all extras at this point. We are only now going to start training your body in more specific ways.

The format for the following chapters will be different from the previous section. I will still describe a structure for each session, but I will include more material on who should use each exercise and how to tailor each exercise for a specific need.

Often, more than one exercise will be described in a chapter. At this stage, it is especially important for you to read the whole chapter before you do any of the exercises, so that you get a feeling for what the exercise is trying to accomplish or what a series of exercises is leading up to. Remember, you are the person who knows the most about how you feel, how your body is responding, and whether you feel comfortable with an exercise or activity. If you read about an exercise and you think, "I don't need this," or, "This is not for me," give it some more thought. It is difficult to get the full flavor of the exercises by reading about them. Your experience of the exercise *could* be quite different from what you anticipate. No matter what your sexual concern or need is, you can benefit and learn something about yourself by doing any of the following exercises.

While the advanced exercises themselves are described for opposite-sex couples, many of them can be adapted for practice by couples of the same sex.

Chapter 10

❤

Exercises for Rapid Ejaculation

The exercises in this chapter are directed toward men who want to experience heightened sexual arousal. They can also be used by men who have a problem with rapid ejaculation. Similar exercises for women are described in the chapter on female arousal.

The core of these exercises is an advanced version of the peaking process. You have already practiced peaking by yourself. Now we will discuss how to do it with a partner. Several separate exercises are described in this chapter: Arousal monitoring, manual and oral peaking, nondemand penetration, intravaginal peaking, plateauing, and keeping your physical and emotional charge together.

Arousal Monitoring

The first step in ejaculation control is arousal monitoring, which you learned to do the section on self-exercises. Now you will do it with your partner.

Think of your sexual arousal on a scale of "1" to "10," with a "1" meaning you are not aroused at all and a "10" meaning you are ejaculating. Remember, this "1" to "10" scale refers to how you *feel,* not your physical response, i.e., not the quality of your erection. For a review of how you may expect to feel at each level, see the chapter, "Exercises to Do by Yourself."

You may have noticed that the more experience you have with peaking, the less you rely on the numbers and the more you rely on your feelings. This is normal and desirable—eventually the numbers should drop out of the process, as you develop a natural awareness of how you feel.

Begin the session with focusing caresses (back caresses) for about ten minutes each. Then you may do a front or genital caress with your partner before you begin the arousal monitoring process.

Assume the passive role and lie on your back. Your partner begins a front caress and moves into the genital caress, as well as oral sex if she desires. She should do these caresses for her own pleasure, as in the early sensate focus exercises. At various points during the caress you should give your partner feedback as to when you feel you are at a "3," "4," "5," "6," "7," "8," and "9" level of arousal.

The first time you monitor your arousal you may not be able to distinguish all the different levels, or they may go by very quickly. You may want to allow yourself to go up two levels at a time; for example, tell your partner when you reach "4," "6," and "8." Each time you tell your partner that you have moved to a higher level of arousal, breathe and relax your muscles. Make sure you are not tightening your PC muscle. Try not to panic or fight off ejaculation. Breathe instead.

At this stage, it doesn't matter how long or short a time you take to reach each level, and it doesn't matter how high you are able to go. The important things are to *focus* on where your partner is touching, *breathe* evenly, and *relax* all of your muscles.

The purpose of this exercise is to become aware of your own sexual response and experience your entire sexual response cycle without interfering with it by moving or holding your breath. If you go all the way through the whole cycle and ejaculate, this is fine. If you are only able to reach what you consider to be a "2" or "3" level of arousal, that's fine too.

If you are the active partner, do the caresses for your own pleasure. As your partner tells you each level he has reached, momentarily stop the caress and then begin again. Do the caresses very slowly, especially the genital caress and oral sex, and especially if your partner has a severe problem with premature ejaculation. It is important for your partner that the stimulation be slow and predictable. Touching slowly will help you focus also. If your partner holds his breath at some point during the caress or tenses his thigh muscles, stop the caress and remind him to relax.

Men, if you are really concerned about premature ejaculation, remember to remain completely passive. Keep your breathing even. Don't hold your breath when your partner touches your abdomen and genitals—focus on the touch. Ask your partner to touch more slowly if you are having trouble focusing. Try not to tense your thigh muscles. It doesn't matter whether your partner is able to touch you for two seconds or twenty minutes before you ejaculate. If you go from level "5" to an ejaculation quickly, this also is fine.

After you do the arousal monitoring the first time, give feedback about whether your partner needs to go more slowly so that you can focus more easily. Remember, we are not yet working on controlling ejaculations, so whatever happens happens. Do not attempt to control your ejaculation at all. Your first impulse when your partner touches your genitals may be to tense up, hold your breath, and think about something else. Tell yourself to relax, and focus on your genital sensations rather than ignore them as you have tried to do in the past.

If you do ejaculate quickly, your partner should give you a front caress for a few minutes and then start over with the arousal monitoring for a few more minutes to give you more practice. Any time you ejaculate quickly during any exercise, the exercise can be begun again after a few minutes.

If you have had a problem with premature ejaculation for some time, you may have begun to feel that ejaculating is not pleasurable. When you feel the point of inevitability, you may experience an "Oh no!" feeling rather than a feeling of strong pleasure and impending release.

Use this arousal monitoring exercise to train yourself to start enjoying your ejaculations again rather than dreading them. From now on, whenever an ejaculation happens in this program, I want you to passively allow yourself to experience it without tensing and without moving. Try to enjoy it *whenever* it happens. It is fine to ejaculate at any time during this program if you feel like doing so. Your eventual ability to learn to ejaculate when you want to will depend on never *trying* to control an ejaculation at any point in this program. Ejaculating during an exercise does not mean that you have somehow "failed" the exercise; if you enjoy an ejaculation whenever it happens, you have done the exercise well.

If you are the partner of a man having problems with premature ejaculation, your impulse may be to become frustrated when you see your partner ejaculate quickly. The best thing you can do to help at this stage, however, is encourage him to enjoy the ejaculation whenever it happens. If your partner ejaculates quickly during any exercise, remember: You can always begin the exercise again after a few minutes.

Do the arousal monitoring exercise as many times as you need to until you can reach and recognize level "7" or "8." It may take two or three or more repetitions until you are confident that you can distinguish how aroused you are. It doesn't matter if you don't have an orgasm during this exercise. What matters is that you leave yourself alone and allow yourself to go at least most of the way through your sexual response cycle without interfering with your own pleasure. If you are having a problem with premature ejaculation, repeat the exercise as many times as you need to until you can do the exercise for ten minutes.

After the exercise, give the same kind of feedback you gave with the other sensate focus exercises. How was your concentration, beginning with the back caresses? Could the man focus as well on the genital caress as he could on the back caress? Was the woman caressing for her own enjoyment? How was your anxiety level? Did either partner feel performance pressure?

Sequence for Arousal Monitoring
Focusing caress — back — First person — 10 minutes
Focusing caress — back — Second person
— 10 minutes
Genital caress — woman passive — 10 minutes
Arousal monitoring — man passive — 15 to 20 minutes
Feedback

Peaking

The purpose of peaking is to bring yourself up to a certain level of arousal and then allow your arousal to subside. Follow the same format as for arousal monitoring, a focusing caress followed by a genital caress by hand or with oral stimulation.

In the first peaking exercise, your partner begins a slow front caress and gradually moves to the genitals. Let her know when you reach level "3," either by saying the number or just saying "Stop." Your partner then moves her caress to some other area of the body until your arousal has dropped one or two points, then begins to caress the genitals again until you report a "4." She then stops and allows the arousal to go down again.

The difference between peaking and arousal monitoring is that during peaking at higher levels, the active person stops and "detumesces" the passive person for a few seconds after each level is reached. "Tumescence" refers to the flow of blood to the genital region. With each successive peak, more blood enters the genitals and you become more aroused (provided that you are breathing and your muscles are relaxed). When each peak is reached, the active partner detumesces the passive partner by ceasing stimulation of the genitals and stroking the abdomen and thighs in the direction away from the genitals. This will cause arousal to go down.

The peaking process may be continued up through "5," "6," "7," "8," "9," and all the way to ejaculation at the final peak if desired. It may be easier to do just the odd levels such as "3," "5," "7," and "9."

Four or five peaks in any one session is enough. You may choose the levels you are comfortable discriminating. You could do one session of peaking at only lower levels—"2," "3," "4," and "5," and then the next session at higher levels—"6," "7," "8," and "9." You can also do a session repeating the same level; for example, you could do a session with all four peaks at level "7."

Remember to remain passive throughout the peaking process. Take a deep breath and relax your leg muscles whenever you feel a surge of arousal. The peaking process will not benefit you if you stay tensed or try to control your ejaculation. Breathe deeply as each new level is reached. Your partner may notice if you are tensing or holding your breath at any point during the peaking process, and can help you by encouraging you to breathe and relax.

Stop between peaks long enough for the arousal to go down about two levels. For example, when you reach "7," have your partner back off and help you detumesce down to around "5." It is just as important for you to get a sense that your arousal is going down as it is for you to get a sense of your arousal going up. The "down-curves" of each peak are as important as the "upcurves," because the downcurves give you the sense that your arousal is controllable if you breathe deeply and stop the stimulation. Remember that the way we recognize our feelings is by contrasting them with the preceding feelings.

Peaking will result in ejaculation control through self-awareness and relaxation, rather than through *working* at controlling your ejaculation. If you have a problem with premature ejaculation, at no point during the peaking process should you be attempting to control your ejaculation. If you feel that you want to control your ejaculation, repeat the arousal monitoring or other earlier exercises until you are more confident of your ability to relax.

If you ejaculate fairly quickly during the peaking process, your partner can do a front caress for a few minutes and then start over. Chances are good that you will experience some level of arousal again. You may need to break the peaking exercise down into separate exercises for manual stimulation and oral stimulation until you become comfortable with each of them.

Do the exercise as many times as you need to until you can easily reach "7" or "8" or until you can passively allow the stimulation for fifteen or twenty minutes. Allow roughly five minutes for each complete peak. It doesn't matter in any peaking session if you have an orgasm, if you ejaculate, or if you have an erection. Continue all the way to orgasm if you can do so without working at it.

You will need to do at least two peaking sessions and possibly more. For the first session, try to distinguish the lower levels—"3," "4," "5," and "6." For the second session, try the higher levels—"5," "6," "7," "8," and "9."

After each peaking session, remember to give feedback about concentration and anxiety. The feedback time is not a time to pick apart your "performance" during the exercise. It is a time to share information about your perceptions of your own concentration and enjoyment, and your perceptions of your own anxiety level and that of your partner.

❤

In another version of peaking, the man becomes active. As your partner strokes your penis or does oral sex, you begin to slowly do pelvic thrusts and pelvic rolls. You will still give your partner feedback about peaks as you reach them.

The movements that you do in this version of the exercise are extremely important. Lie on your back as your partner strokes your genitals, and do any type of slow pelvic thrust or roll that you wish, as long as you do not tighten your stomach, thigh, or hip muscles. Slowly thrust your penis against your partner's hand or mouth. When you reach a peak, stop moving, breathe, and relax your muscles. Your partner can help you tell if you are tensing your stomach, hips, or thighs as you thrust.

Here are the sequences for the three peaking sessions. After you have done these a couple of times, you will have a sense of which levels may be a problem for you, and you can do another session to practice those levels.

Sequence for Peaking — Low Levels
Focusing caress — First person — 10 minutes
Focusing caress — Second person — 10 minutes
Genital caress — woman passive — 10 minutes
Peaking — man passive — "3," "4," "5," "6"
— 15 to 20 minutes
Feedback

Sequence for Peaking — High Levels
Focusing caress — First person — 10 minutes
Focusing caress — Second person — 10 minutes
Genital caress — woman passive — 10 minutes
Peaking — man passive — "5," "6," "7," "8," "9," "10" if
possible — 15 to 20 minutes
Feedback

Sequence for Peaking — Man Active
Focusing caress — First person — 10 minutes
Focusing caress — Second person — 10 minutes
Genital caress — woman passive — 10 minutes
Peaking — man active — "5," "6," "7," "8," "9," "10" if
possible — 15 to 20 minutes
Feedback

Nondemand Penetration

The peaking process continues from hand and oral stimulation through intercourse. Before you begin intravaginal peaking, however, I would like you to experience your first episode of nondemand intercourse.

There are two forms of nondemand intercourse—flaccid insertion, and the "quick dip." Use the quick dip if you tend to have strong erections. Use flaccid insertion if you tend to have less strong erections.

For the quick dip version of the exercise, you add a quick episode of intercourse onto the end of a manual or oral peaking exercise. Do not use the quick dip until the man has experience with peaking by hand or oral stimulation at "8" or "9." The reason for the quick dip is not to practice lasting during intercourse. In fact, you probably will ejaculate immediately. The purpose of the quick dip is to allow you to enjoy your ejaculation as much as you can.

If you are aroused after a peaking session and have peaked up to "8" or "9," go ahead and have your partner get on top of your penis. Try to stay as passive as possible and let your partner do the thrusting. Focus on the penis inside the vagina, breathe, and relax your leg muscles.

It doesn't matter how long you last before ejaculating. This isn't a test to see how long you can hold out. It is a form of nondemand intercourse, a way for you and your partner to experience heightened arousal. Peaking prior to ejaculation will make your ejaculation stronger and more enjoyable when it happens. In a later chapter, we will see that peaking can make a woman's orgasm stronger and more enjoyable also.

If you choose the flaccid insertion version of nondemand penetration, start with focusing caresses such as back caresses. Then do one or two low level peaks ("3" or "4") by hand with the man passive. Then the partners should assume a side by side or "scissors" position. The man should lie on his right side. The woman should lie on her back at a right angle to him with her left leg on top of his leg and her right leg between his legs.

Move closer to each other so that your genitals are touching. Use baby oil on the penis and on the vagina. Rest the penis up against the vaginal opening. Both partners should then breathe deeply and relax their muscles while the penis and vagina are in contact with each other.

Both partners should focus on the level of arousal they feel from this contact. If the arousal level is less than "5" or so, move your genitals even closer together so there is more stimulation. Focus on the stimulation, breathe, relax, and tell your partner your arousal level. You may need to let this arousal peak go back down for a minute. This is fine.

When the man's arousal level is below "5" again, the woman should partially insert the penis into the vagina. Make sure you use plenty of lubrication. If the man does not have a full erection, gently fold or stuff the penis inside. Then breathe and relax your leg muscles again. Tell each other your arousal levels. When the arousal has dropped one or two levels, insert the whole penis into the vagina. Breathe and relax. Neither partner should move or thrust. Be aware of your arousal level. Don't try to control an ejaculation. If you feel like ejaculating, go ahead.

For this exercise, it doesn't matter how much of the penis goes in, how long it stays in, whether it stays erect, whether the man has an ejaculation, or whether the woman has an orgasm. Just relax and experience the feelings, whether they last a few seconds or a few minutes.

After a few minutes of penetration without moving, start to move slowly if you are both comfortable. Don't try to control an ejaculation, and don't worry if your erection or arousal goes down. What is important in this exercise is that you don't pressure yourself, and you allow yourself to experience feelings of the penis inside the vagina while remaining comfortable. If you do ejaculate, leave the penis inside the vagina and continue to experience the feelings for a few more minutes.

Sequence for Nondemand Penetration
(Flaccid Insertion)
Focusing caress — First person — 10 minutes
Focusing caress — Second person — 10 minutes
Genital caress — man passive
— 10 minutes (one or two peaks)
Nondemand penetration — 1 to 15 minutes
Feedback

❤

Before I describe how to peak inside the vagina, I would like to say one thing about premature ejaculation in general. Many men feel that they ejaculate too fast, when in fact the time they spend inside the vagina is probably longer than average. I believe the average amount of time an American man spends during actual intercourse is somewhere between four and eight minutes. By using the exercises in this book, you *will* learn to have intercourse for a longer period of time. However, after you have experienced the exercises, you may feel that the level of arousal you reach is much more important than how long you can last. The vaginal peaking exercises will teach how to have intercourse at higher levels of arousal without trying to contain your sexual charge or push it away.

Intravaginal Peaking

Begin as usual with a focusing caress (either back or face) to relax yourselves and promote sensual arousal. The man may then do a front or genital caress with his partner.

Vaginal peaking may be done in the side by side position or with the woman on top. Either way, the man remains as passive as possible and lets the woman control the movement. I will describe the exercise with the woman on top.

The man lies on his back. The woman does a front caress, a genital caress, and nondemand oral sex if she likes. She should do the caresses for her own pleasure, as always. Next, she peaks the man manually or orally up to about level "5" or "6," with the man providing verbal feedback. She then inserts the penis into her vagina and remains motionless for a few moments. Both partners should take deep breaths and relax their leg muscles.

The woman then starts to move *very slowly*. Both partners should be focusing on the sensations, as always. The man provides feedback about higher levels of arousal including "7," "8," "9," and "10" if he reaches it. At each peak, the woman may either stop moving in order to allow the man to detumesce, or she may withdraw the penis completely.

Each peak should take about five minutes, as in manual peaking. However, the peaks may be much shorter the first time you do this exercise. It may take several experiences with intravaginal peaking before the man is completely able to breathe and relax with the penetration.

As with the previous exercises, there are no performance demands. It doesn't matter if the man ejaculates immediately or loses his erection, or if the woman has an orgasm. If you feel you are at "9," or if you feel an ejaculation approaching, tell your partner, open your eyes, relax, and take a deep breath. Enjoy the ejaculation.

If the man ejaculates after five minutes or less, wait a few minutes and start the exercise over again. If the erection goes down, the woman should resume nondemand oral sex or genital caressing with verbal feedback from the man, and then insert the penis again. If the woman has an orgasm, she should just experience it and continue to thrust as slowly as possible. An impending orgasm is not a reason to stop the exercise or to start to move faster. Maintain your concentration—it may be difficult, but this type of mental and physical discipline is both possible and enjoyable.

Repeat the first vaginal peaking exercise until the man can last ten to fifteen minutes with slow thrusting by the woman. If you have a severe problem with premature ejaculation, you will need to repeat this exercise several times, with the woman moving more each time. You need to learn to focus, relax and breathe with this exercise the same way you did with manual or oral peaking.

Sequence for Vaginal Peaking with Woman Active
Focusing caress — First person — 10 minutes
Focusing caress — Second person — 10 minutes
Genital caress/oral sex — man active — 10 minutes
Peaking — woman active (front caress, genital caress,
oral sex, penetration, peaking "5," "6," "7," "8,"
"9," "10") — 15 to 30 minutes
Feedback

After the man becomes confident with his ability to peak vaginally with the woman active, he may become more active. Eventually we will switch complete control of the peaking process over to the man.

Begin as before with focusing caresses. The woman then begins a genital caress or oral sex. The man lies on his back. The woman climbs on top and inserts the penis at a comfortable "5" or "6" level and then holds still.

The man at this point will control the speed and timing of the thrusting. He should peak at "6," "7," "8," "9," and "10" if possible. It is not necessary for him to tell his partner when he has reached each level; at this stage, he may internally monitor the sensations and stop when necessary.

This is a crucial exercise for men with premature ejaculation problems, because it may be tempting to thrust the way you have in the past. This thrusting technique was probably too fast and too deep, with a tendency to hold the breath and tighten the leg muscles. When you begin to thrust during this exercise, do so as slowly as possible. Thrust your penis by using pelvic rolls rather than by using your legs. Focus on caressing the inside of the vagina with your penis. If possible, try to move your penis inside the vagina while keeping your other body muscles (such as those in your stomach, legs, and buttocks) as relaxed as possible. Maintain a constant rate of breathing throughout the exercise, even when you ejaculate. Do this version of the peaking exercise until you are comfortable with it for fifteen minutes or so.

Sequence for Vaginal Peaking with Man Active
Focusing caress — First person — 10 minutes
Focusing caress — Second person — 10 minutes
Genital caress/oral sex — man active (optional)
— 10 minutes
Peaking — "6," "7," "8," "9," "10" (woman on top,
man active) — 15 to 20 minutes
Feedback

❤

Now you are ready to try vaginal peaking with the man on top. In order to maintain continuity and promote relaxation, begin with focusing caresses. The woman peaks the passive man up to about "5" or "6" and then climbs on top of the penis.

Do one or two comfortable peaks with the woman on top and then switch to the following position, with which you may not be familiar. It is a position with the man on top that is used in sex therapy because it allows maximum relaxation of most of the body, and it also allows the maximum amount of stimulation for both partners.

The woman lies on her back with a pillow under her buttocks. She bends her knees, puts her legs up in the air, and spreads them. (Support your legs with your arms if you need to.) The man then kneels, sitting back on his heels, keeping his penis as close to the vagina as possible. He supports his body weight with his legs, not his arms. Leaning forward on your arms at this point will distract you from your feelings of arousal and will put unnecessary stress on your body. You may provide additional support for your weight by grasping your partner's thighs. This position puts your center of gravity in your pelvis and legs rather than in your chest or arms. (In Indian sex manuals this position is called the *shulanka,* or "trident" position, because the man's body is vertical with the woman's legs in the air on either side.)

The man inserts his penis and begins to thrust—slowly. You literally cannot do this exercise too slowly. Use plenty of lubrication. The woman remains passive while her partner peaks up to "5," "6," "7," "8," "9," and "10" if possible.

Move your penis in and out of the vagina by rolling or rocking your pelvis rather than by tensing your legs. Take about five minutes for each peak. As you reach each peak, you can either stop moving, slow down, or withdraw completely. At each peak, breathe deeply and relax your leg muscles.

During this exercise, practice your sensate focus techniques. Think of yourself as caressing your partner's vagina with your penis.

The point of insertion is usually the most crucial point, as it is the point of highest anxiety. You may need to practice inserting and removing the penis several times while relaxing, breathing, and focusing. Thrust slowly, and at each peak, either slow down or stop until your arousal goes down. Focus, breathe, and relax. You may either tell your partner how aroused you are or keep track for yourself. If you reach orgasm, enjoy yourself.

Practice vaginal peaking with the man on top until you can do it for ten to fifteen minutes.

One word of caution about this and other peaking exercises: It *is* possible to overpeak. Doing more than about five or six high-level peaks in a row may result in a temporary inability to ejaculate when you want to. There is nothing harmful or abnormal about this, so do not put pressure on yourself in any way. Your ability to ejaculate will return in a few minutes. If you reach "9" and cannot ejaculate, just end the exercise.

Sequence for Vaginal Peaking
with Man Active and on Top
Focusing caress — First person — 10 minutes
Focusing caress — Second person — 10 minutes
Vaginal peaking — front caress and genital caress,
woman active — peaking with man on top, man active
("5," "6," "7," "8," "9," "10" levels) — 15 to 30 minutes
Feedback

❤

For the next peaking exercise, you may begin intercourse with the man on top. Don't forget the focusing caresses to promote relaxation first, and the woman may do a genital caress with her partner if he needs some stimulation to have an erection.

In these final peaking exercises, the woman should begin to move as she normally would during intercourse. The man can tell the woman how aroused he is and if or when she needs to stop moving or can move faster. You can also try other positions for peaking at this stage, such as the rear-entry position or a side by side position.

Plateauing

Plateauing is similar to peaking, except that when you reach a certain level of arousal, you hold yourself at that level by fine-tuning your focusing, breathing, and movement. Begin plateauing with your partner after you are completely comfortable with vaginal peaking with the man on top.

The first plateauing session is done with the man on top. Do focusing caresses and nondemand genital caresses or oral sex first. The partners should then move into the position described earlier for vaginal peaking, with the woman on her back and the man kneeling.

For your first plateau, attempt to stay at level "6" or "7." Insert the penis and begin to slowly thrust until you feel you are at "6." Continue to focus, breathe, and relax. The instant you feel yourself go beyond "6," stop or slow down until you are below "6." Then start moving again.

By adjusting the speed of your thrusting and taking deep breaths, you may be able to plateau at "6" for a minute or two. Eventually you will be able to maintain yourself at a constant level by stopping, starting, or changing the speed or angle of your thrusting. Use the types of movements that you practiced when you did the plateauing exercise by yourself. Switch your focus from the head of your penis to the base, to the sides, or to the walls of your partner's vagina. Remember to caress the vagina with your penis. When you feel your arousal build, breathe deeply and relax your leg muscles.

As with the peaking, it is possible to "overplateau." If it starts to become work, switch your mode of thought to enjoyment and just go ahead and enjoy yourself, after letting your partner know that the exercise is over.

Try the plateauing exercise at "8" or even "9." For fun, see how long you can hold yourself at the brink of orgasm by breathing and relaxing your body muscles (not by squeezing your PC muscle). Even at this stage, you still should not be doing anything to try to control an ejaculation, and you should not be "working at it."

Sequence for Plateauing
Focusing caress — First person — 10 minutes
Focusing caress — Second person — 10 minutes
Plateauing — man active, man on top ("6," "7," "8," or "9" level) — 15 to 30 minutes
Feedback

Keeping Your Emotional and Physical Charge Together

Keeping your emotional and physical charge together is an exercise that is especially helpful for flaccid ejaculation. Remember that flaccid ejaculation is a problem in which the man ejaculates before he has a full erection. It is a combination of premature ejaculation and erection problems.

I have mentioned earlier that there are really two different arousal scales for men. There is the "1" to "10" scale of your internal feeling of closeness to ejaculation (we can call this your emotional charge), and there is the "1" to "10" scale of how hard your erection is (we can call this your physical charge).

So far, you have only been using the first scale. I now want you to become aware of the second scale. Normally a man's physical and emotional charge run parallel, with the erection becoming harder as he becomes more aroused. It is not unusual, though, for these two responses to be a little bit off; for example, your erection could be at "8" and you could be ejaculating, or your feeling of arousal could be at "6" and yet you could have a very strong erection.

In flaccid ejaculation, these two responses have gotten completely out of line. For example, the emotional charge may be at "10" while the physical charge is only at "3" or "4" (not really erect enough for easy penetration).

If you are having flaccid ejaculations you should do the vaginal peaking in a side by side position, gently folding or stuffing the penis into the vagina. After you have learned to control your ejaculation by focusing, breathing, relaxing, and peaking, do the following exercise in which you attempt to keep your physical and emotional sexual arousal together.

Begin the session with focusing caresses, then do a nondemand genital caress with your partner if you like.

The man then lies on his back while the woman caresses his genitals or does oral sex. The man asks the woman to stop for a few seconds whenever he feels his emotional charge go higher than his physical charge.

You may also do this exercise during intercourse, with the man on top. The woman lies on her back, knees bent and legs up in the air and spread apart. The man then kneels and begins to stroke the vaginal lips with his penis. Use plenty of lubrication.

As you caress the outside of your partner's vagina with your penis, you will be aware that you are reaching a certain level of emotional arousal. If you feel that your physical arousal (your erection) is lower than your emotional charge, slow down. Use your penis to caress some other part of your partner's body until your emotional charge is back down to the same level as your physical charge. Then begin to stroke the vagina again.

Continue stroking either outside or inside the vagina, but every time you feel that your emotional charge has gone beyond your physical charge, slow down, breathe, relax, and change the sort of stimulation you are receiving until the physical and emotional levels are the same again.

You cannot will your erection to become harder so

that it matches your emotional charge, but you can lower your emotional charge to match your erection level by slowing your movement, breathing, focusing, and relaxing. Do four or five "peaks" this way. Spend about fifteen minutes on this exercise.

You will find that each time your emotional charge reduces to come into line with your erection level, the erection level will increase with the next peak. Ejaculate at the end of the exercise if you feel like it. You may need to repeat this exercise several times or alternate it with a peaking exercise until you begin to notice definite changes in the hardness of your erections.

Sequence for Keeping Your Physical and
Emotional Charge Together
Focusing caress — First person — 10 minutes
Focusing caress — Second person — 10 minutes
Front and genital caress — man active — 10 minutes
Charge exercise — man passive — 15 to 20 minutes
Feedback

or

Focusing caress — First person — 10 minutes
Focusing caress — Second person — 10 minutes
Front and genital caress — man active — 10 minutes
Charge exercise — man active — 15 to 20 minutes
Feedback

❤

The peaking and plateauing exercises, done in a relaxed manner, will give you the foundation for ejaculation control because they eliminate anxiety and performance pressure. The exercise for keeping your physical and emotional charge together requires intense focus and can add a completely new dimension to your sexual awareness.

Chapter 11

❤

Exercises for Erection Problems

If you have been working on enhancing your erections, the basic sensate focus exercises in Part II probably helped you quite a bit. If you have been experiencing erection problems, and if your partner has been able to do genital caresses and oral sex in a nondemand way for her own pleasure, chances are good that you are beginning to have satisfying erections.

The biggest barrier to successful erections is the habit of trying to become active sexually before your body is ready. Your erection problems may stem from not allowing your body to become fully aroused before you attempt to have intercourse, or the fact that you have not paid attention to age-related changes in your body's capacity for erections. You may not be getting erections at all because you are cognitively monitoring sensations, rather than experiencing them. Or you may be allowing yourself to become somewhat erect, but then you may panic when you feel the erection start to go down.

The exercises described in this chapter deal with these concerns, and they also deal with some of the myths about the importance of erections. The exercises are: Flaccid insertion, erection awareness, getting and losing erections, and maintaining erections during intercourse.

Flaccid Insertion

You may have been getting partial erections but avoided using them for intercourse because you thought they weren't "hard enough." The purpose of this exercise (also called "quiet vagina" or "stuffing") is to dispel the myth that your penis has to be rock-hard in order to have intercourse.

Flaccid insertion was described in the previous chapter in the section on nondemand penetration. I am repeating the complete instructions for the exercise here because flaccid insertion is even more important for erection problems.

Begin with focusing caresses as usual. Then, you may do a genital caress or oral sex with your female partner. For the stuffing exercise, it is easiest to use the "scissors" position. The man should lie on his right side. The woman lies on her back at a right angle to the man. She puts her left leg on top of his legs and her right leg between his legs. Then the partners scoot up against each other so that their genitals are touching.

Both partners should breathe and relax. The woman should then caress the man's genitals and her own genitals with some lubricant. Both partners focus on this caress. If the man becomes erect or partially erect, that is fine. No matter what the state of erection, the woman then gently folds or stuffs the flaccid or partially erect penis into her vagina. The woman should open her vagina with her fingers. It is sometimes helpful to slide the flaccid penis into the vagina by using one or two fingers as a splint. Rather than trying to insert the tip of the penis first, place the penis along the vaginal lips with the base of the penis at the vaginal opening. Then gently push on the base of the penis to insert it. The tip will follow. The woman should then squeeze her PC muscle to make sure that the penis is inside.

The purpose of this exercise is not to become aroused, but to experience the feeling of being inside the vagina with no pressure to have an erection or perform sexually. Once the penis is inside the vagina, it will be tempting to move or thrust. The first time you do this exercise, try to remain as motionless as possible. Breathe and relax your legs. At most, squeeze your PC muscle a few times to assure yourselves that you are still inserted. Practice breathing, focusing, and keeping all your muscles relaxed while you are inside. Even if you become erect while inside, don't move. Do this for fifteen to thirty minutes, then stop and give each other feedback.

In your next session, repeat the entire exercise. This time the man may begin to slowly move his penis inside his partner's vagina, whether he has an erection or not. Think of this as caressing your partner's vagina with your penis. If you become aware that your erection is going down, move more slowly or stop completely. Breathe and relax. Both partners should focus completely on the sensations in the penis and vagina. It is easier to focus if you move slowly.

Practice the flaccid insertion exercise as many times as you need to, with progressively more and more movement, until you are comfortable with the idea that you can be inside the vagina whenever you want to, no matter how hard or soft you are. Do the exercise until you can truly allow yourself to relax and leave yourself alone no matter how hard or soft you are.

Sequence for Flaccid Insertion
Focusing caress — First person — 10 minutes
Focusing caress — Second person — 10 minutes
Front and genital caress — man active — 10 minutes
Flaccid insertion — 15 to 30 minutes
— side by side position
Feedback

Erection Awareness

The flaccid insertion exercise will help you overcome the idea that your penis must meet certain standards of hardness for intercourse. Sometimes men have a different problem, which is that they actually do not know whether their penis is hard or not. This may sound hard to believe, but it can happen if you have ignored the sensations in your body for a long time.

The basic sensate focus exercises helped you learn to experience feelings in your genitals. If you have a problem with erection awareness, you may experience pleasant feelings, but you still may not be aware that your penis is hard enough for intercourse. I have worked with clients who had this problem; I would do a genital caress for twenty minutes or so and the client would have an erection for almost the whole time without realizing it. Eventually the erection would go away simply because so much time had elapsed. The client would think that in fact he had not had an erection at all during the session! (This is similar to insomniacs who complain that they are not getting any sleep, when in fact they are sleeping several hours a night and don't know it.)

Another reason for lack of erection awareness is that sometimes a man specifically learns to ignore his erections because he thinks that is the best way to *get* an erection. Actually, he is partially on the right track. What he needs to do is stop *worrying* about his genitals and start *feeling* them. The feelings of arousal in your genitals are something you definitely want to concentrate on, not ignore!

To practice erection awareness with a partner, think of the hardness of your erection on a scale from "1" to "10." Level "1" would be a completely flaccid penis, and "10" would be an extremely hard, almost painful, erection. If you get erections in the morning or when you masturbate, practice describing them using this scale.

Begin your first erection awareness exercise with focusing caresses. Then you may do a genital caress or nondemand oral sex with your partner, after which you should lie back with your eyes closed.

Women, you will monitor this exercise. Begin a nondemand front caress and continue to a genital caress or oral sex for about twenty minutes. Ask your partner at various points during the caress how strong he thinks his erection is. If his estimate differs significantly from your estimate, have him open his eyes and look at his penis.

If your partner describes his erection as "2" when in fact it is hard enough for intercourse (about "5"), he needs to believe this. After he has seen the erection, have him close his eyes again and concentrate on the feelings in his penis so that he can learn to recognize these feelings without having to look.

It is important to make sure that your partner breathes evenly and remains relaxed during this exercise. If your partner holds his breath, remind him to breathe. If he tenses his leg muscles, lightly pinch them or tap them as a signal to relax. If he squeezes his PC muscle, remind him to relax it. As always, if he starts to become anxious or starts working at it, caress another body part to take the focus off the genitals. If your partner finds it impossible to relax, back up to an exercise with which he felt comfortable, like a back caress or an upper-body front caress. Men, do the erection awareness exercise as many times as you need to until you are confident you can recognize, through feeling alone, when your erection is sufficient for penetration.

Sequence for Erection Awareness
Focusing caress — First person — 10 minutes
Focusing caress — Second person — 10 minutes
Front and genital caress — man active, woman passive
— 10 minutes
Erection awareness exercise — woman active,
man passive — 15 to 20 minutes
Feedback

Getting and Losing Erections

The physiology of having and maintaining an erection is complex and well beyond the scope of this book. Let's talk about it in simple terms. Think about your partner doing a genital caress or some oral sex with you. When you are breathing deeply and evenly, and not holding your breath, she will be able to feel (or even see) blood flow into your penis. If you hold your breath, she will be able to feel blood flow back out. If you keep your abdomen, thigh, and buttocks muscles completely relaxed, she will be able to feel blood flow into your penis. The instant you tighten up, she will be able to feel the blood flow back out. If you keep your PC muscle relaxed, blood will flow in. If you either consciously or unconsciously squeeze your PC muscle, blood will flow back out. This simple in-and-out process, which your partner can easily observe, will be the basis of the next erection exercise.

"What goes up must come down." We all accept this law of gravity in the abstract. However, when it comes to erections, many men believe—or hope—that "What goes up should stay up forever!" It is perfectly normal for erections *to get harder and softer several times during the course of a sexual encounter.* When men feel their erection start to get soft (whether it is during intercourse or before), they often panic and start frenzied activities to try to regain the erection or to "use it before they lose it." Working at it or trying to keep it hard is the worst thing you can do, as it virtually guarantees that you will lose the erection.

If you are one of those men who panics when an erection starts to go down, you need to learn a new response to this situation. Your previous response has been, "Oh no, I'm losing it! I need to *hurry up* and *do something* with it before it goes down completely!" Guess what? What you really need to do is exactly the opposite.

You have learned to believe that once you lose an erection, it will never come back. It is obvious how you learned this—in previous situations when you lost an erection, you worried about it, and this guaranteed that it never came back.

Whenever you get that panicked feeling because you are losing an erection, you need to use that feeling as a signal to tell yourself the *opposite:* "I'm losing it! I need to relax and enjoy the sensations in my penis. I need to make sure that I don't try to work at anything sexual when I am feeling anxious. I need to take a deep breath, relax my leg muscles, and focus on how my partner is touching me."

Some men experience a more extreme reaction, called "pelvic steal syndrome." In this case, the man can get an erection but loses it as soon as he starts to move his large muscles or tighten them up. The larger muscles (especially the leg muscles) literally steal the blood away from the erection. This is a complex phenomenon, and there is some debate over whether it can be cured by anything other than surgical means. I believe it is, and I have seen clients improve with the exercise I will describe.

The "get-and-lose" exercise will help you practice a

new response when you feel your erection go down. You will learn that "what goes down must come up."

Begin the exercise as you would any other session, with a focusing caress. Then you may do a nondemand front or genital caress with the man active. After that, the man lies on his back with his eyes closed. The woman then begins a nondemand front caress, genital caress, and oral sex. As always, she does the caresses for her own pleasure, and she should note whether the man is breathing evenly and relaxing.

Whenever the man gets a noticeable erection response, the woman should stop the stimulation and allow the erection to go all the way back down. Then she should start over with the caressing and allow the erection to come back up again. Repeat this as many times as possible within a twenty minute to half-hour period.

The first time you do this exercise, it may be frustrating. In fact, the first time you do it, you may not have an erection at all because you will be worrying about it. If you do have an erection, it may be tempting to think your old thoughts or go back to your old habits of flexing your PC muscle, tensing your thighs, thrusting your pelvis, or holding your breath when you feel yourself losing the erection. Your partner can give you feedback about whether you are doing these things. She can help you monitor this so that you become aware of the simple relationships: Relaxing equals blood flowing in, tensing equals blood flowing out.

Many men develop a habit of tensing their PC muscle group as they are becoming aroused. Tightening your PC muscle may make you feel as if you are "pumping up" your erection, but in fact it has the opposite effect—it will cause your erection to go down. An especially negative habit is tensing and holding the area of your PC muscle that includes the anal sphincter. This can cause you to lose your erection quickly. Make sure that you keep your anal sphincter completely relaxed during any sensate focus exercise, especially those involving genital stimulation.

The get-and-lose exercise should demonstrate the relationships between muscle tension and erection response quite clearly. You will learn that if you relax, your erection will return, whereas if you become tense or work at it, your penis will stay soft.

This exercise will also give you a chance to practice your new responses to the former panic situation. During the first few erection losses you will probably experience frustration and worry. Tell your partner what you are feeling and have her coach you on relaxing when you feel your erection going down. Do this exercise as many times as you need to, until you honestly are completely comfortable with feeling that your erection is going down.

If you were not having frequent morning erections before you began this program, the blood flow system in your penis is probably literally out of shape. The self-caressing exercises will help this. You may need to do the get-and-lose exercise several times.

Relearning your erection response is a gradual process. Your erections will not spring up to level "10" overnight, especially if there have been physiological problems and your circulatory system needs to get back in shape. Each time you do an exercise, you will notice more erection response.

Sequence for Getting and Losing Erections
Focusing caress — First person — 10 minutes
Focusing caress — Second person — 10 minutes
Front and genital caress — man active — 10 minutes
Get-and-lose exercise — woman active
— 15 to 20 minutes
Feedback

Maintaining Erections During Intercourse

Suppose that you successfully have erections and intercourse with the exercises described so far. What should you do if you feel yourself start to lose your erection after you have been having intercourse for some time?

It is perfectly normal for your erection to get harder and softer while you are having intercourse. For example, you may penetrate with a level "6" erection, feel it go up to "8," then back to "7," and so forth. If you feel your erection start to go down, the secret is not to panic. Use the techniques that you practiced in the get-and-lose erection exercise. Do not immediately start to thrust harder or faster or become more active. Instead, breathe, relax your legs, focus your attention on the feelings in your penis, and start to move *more slowly.*

The reason you lost your erection in the first place was probably that you were becoming distracted. Ask yourself what is distracting you. Are you thinking about something other than sex, for example, work? Sensate focus is the answer to distracting thoughts of this type. Is your erection going down because you are tired and feel that you have had intercourse for a long enough time? Remember not to put pressure on yourself. Do not continue intercourse if it no longer feels good, and do not attempt to have an orgasm if you really don't feel like it.

Another option if you are concerned about losing erections during intercourse is to go through the peaking process with your partner, as described in the chapter on exercises for rapid ejaculation. The peaking exercises can help you become more aroused and stay more aroused during intercourse, which will help you maintain your erection. If you began the program being unable to get erections, you may be losing erections during intercourse now because you are having intercourse for a longer amount of time than your body is used to. If so, knowing how to peak during intercourse will help you become aroused enough to ejaculate before you become tired and lose your erection. You can then use the peaking process to learn to last longer without becoming fatigued.

If you know how to peak and you still have trouble maintaining erections during intercourse, try this erection maintenance exercise. You are going to *think* your erection back up using intense sensate focus.

Be sure you are having intercourse in a comfortable position and not a position that is putting stress on your chest and arms. When you feel your erection go down, breathe, relax your legs, stop all movement for a moment, and focus your attention completely on the feelings in your penis.

Slowly begin to caress the inside of your partner's vagina with your penis, making movements that are just barely vigorous enough for you to feel. Feel the warmth surrounding the different areas of your penis. Start with the slowest possible discernible movement and gradually increase the speed as your erection grows. It may also be helpful to think of this in terms of your partner using the inside of her vagina to caress the different parts of your penis.

Instead of relying on your partner to give you some kind of stimulation in order to get an erection, you are mentally providing your own stimulation by a combination of intense sensate focus and barely perceptible movements. For this exercise to be enjoyable, both partners should focus all their attention on the feelings in the penis and vagina. Take turns moving, or move at the same time.

The erection maintenance exercise can be done as a separate exercise in any position. It is easiest to do in a side by side position, or with the man kneeling in front of the woman (the "trident" position described earlier).

If you use the trident position, start the exercise without an erection. Kneel in front of the woman and begin to caress her vaginal lips with your penis. Breathe, relax your muscles, and focus totally on the sensations in your penis. Use a masturbation motion if it helps you focus. Insert the penis when you have a moderate erection. Stop and allow the erection to go down. Then *slowly* start to move and focus until you are aware that the erection has returned. Thrust by rolling your pelvis rather than by tightening your leg muscles.

This is similar to peaking, except that you are using the physical response scale instead of the emotional response scale. Your partner should remain passive while you practice allowing your erection to go up and down. She should focus intensely on her feelings in order to get the maximum sensual enjoyment from the exercise.

Sequence for Erection Maintenance
Focusing caress — First person — 10 minutes
Focusing caress — Second person — 10 minutes
Front and genital caress — man active — 10 minutes
Maintenance exercise — man active — 15 to 20 minutes
Feedback

Chapter 12

❤

Exercises for Female Arousal

The exercises in this chapter are for women who want to become more easily aroused or have orgasms through intercourse. The exercises you did by yourself and the basic sensate focus exercises have probably helped you quite a bit already. In addition, if you have done any of the peaking or erection exercises in Chapters 10 and 11 with your partner, you no doubt received sensual and sexual enjoyment from those. The exercises in this chapter are variations on the peaking and plateauing processes. Before we begin, I would like to share some thoughts with you about female arousal and female orgasms.

There has been some controversy in the past about how women have orgasms (or even whether they have them at all). According to early psychoanalysts, orgasms resulting from stimulation of the clitoris were in some way more "immature" than orgasms originating in the vagina. Research conducted by Masters and Johnson indicated that all orgasms resulted from clitoral stimulation and there was no such thing as a vaginal orgasm.

More recent research indicates that there are a number of ways that women can have orgasms. Some women experience orgasm with no physical stimulation at all. For example, you may awaken from a sexy dream and find you are having an orgasm. (Interestingly, the more a man has sex, the less likely he is to experience a wet dream. However, the more often a woman has sex and the more satisfying it is, the more likely she is to experience dreams that involve orgasm.) Other women may experience orgasm through stimulation of the breasts. Clitoral stimulation commonly produces orgasm, and so does extended stimulation of the outer third of the vagina, including the PC muscle. As mentioned, the PC muscle is the muscle that spasms rhythmically during orgasm, and stimulating it can often trigger the orgasm.

Many sites within the vagina can produce orgasm. One is the G spot, discussed earlier. In some women, stimulation of the G spot can produce the release of a fluid. This is called female ejaculation, or a "gusher." Another sensitive site is the cul-de-sac, which is the area behind the cervix at the end of the vagina. Stimulation of the cervix with the penis may also be pleasurable and may result in orgasm.

An orgasm will feel like this. The muscles around your uterus and cervix will spasm so that your abdomen will suck in. You may expel some air from your vagina. Your PC muscle will flutter. Your neck, arms, and legs may spasm involuntarily. If this happens, just let it happen. You may feel a tingling sensation in some parts of your body, and a sensation of warmth that moves from your genitals up to your chest, neck, and face. If you have fair skin, your face, neck, and chest may flush.

With so many possible ways in which women can have orgasms, why do current surveys of sexual behavior indicate that many women are not experiencing orgasms? Especially given the recent findings on sites in which orgasms may be triggered, there is theoretically no reason why any woman should not be able to have an orgasm with the stimulation of intercourse.

What do you need to do in order to learn to have orgasms through intercourse? First, you may need to change some of your attitudes. You need to believe that it can happen. You need to take responsibility for having the orgasm instead of depending on your partner to "give" you one. You also need to give yourself permission to take pleasure for yourself and not worry about your partner.

You may also need to experiment with more stimulating behaviors than you have used in the past. If you are currently not experiencing orgasms when you want to during intercourse, there is nothing wrong with you. It is more likely that the stimulation you have been receiving has not been the type of stimulation that is likely to trigger an orgasm.

When men are adolescents, they usually have quite a bit of practice with masturbation, and they learn to stimulate themselves very effectively. (Sometimes they learn to stimulate themselves *too* effectively and find that they have little ejaculatory control when they are with a woman.) Women, however, often do not learn effective stimulation techniques and are more likely to rely on their partner to know how to stimulate them.

Many women even have difficulty knowing *when* they are physically aroused. For example, in a recent psychological study, female college students had measuring devices placed in their vaginas and were shown erotic movies. They were then asked to rate how physically aroused they were at various times during the movies. The results showed that the women did not have a good idea of when they were lubricating or when their vaginal tissues were swelling—both signs of sexual arousal.

Another problem is that many couples only have intercourse in the missionary position, in which the woman lies flat on her back with her legs straight out and the man lies on top of her. Of all the ways you could have intercourse, this is probably the least likely position for allowing the woman to easily have an orgasm. Why? It is difficult if not impossible to move your pelvis, your genitals are tucked up under you, and the only way you can thrust is to tense your leg muscles and move up and down. We know from the material on male arousal that when you tense those leg muscles, not only are you "working at it," but you are also stealing blood away from your genitals. If you are already extremely aroused, it is possible to have an orgasm in that position, but it is unlikely.

In the exercises in this chapter, you will learn to recognize your psychological arousal on a scale of "1" to "10." Becoming more aware of your *psychological* sense of sensual and sexual arousal will in turn help you become more aware of your *physical* arousal.

This chapter will also describe arousing positions and activities. However, whether a woman has an orgasm during intercourse probably depends as much on relaxation and timing of the stimulation as it does on the type of stimulation.

Arousal Monitoring

You have already learned to monitor your arousal, to peak, and to plateau in the chapter on exercises you did by yourself. The first exercise you do with a partner will be arousal monitoring.

Begin with focusing caresses, followed by a non-demand front or genital caress with your partner, if you wish. Then lie comfortably on your back with your arms at your sides and your legs spread. Place a pillow under your buttocks if this is more comfortable. The man then begins a slow sensate focus front and genital caress. He may include oral sex. He should remember to take pleasure for himself and to move as slowly as possible. Men, the way to make sure that your partner enjoys herself and receives the maximum amount of stimulation is for you to focus totally on what you are doing and enjoy yourself.

Women, tell your partner when you reach different levels of arousal. You will be familiar with these levels from doing the self-caressing exercises. If you need to review what the different arousal levels feel like, refer back to that chapter.

Focus exactly on what your partner is doing. If you are uncomfortable or anxious in any way, ask him to move more slowly. If you feel he is "working at it," ask him to move more slowly. When you feel your arousal increase, take a deep breath and relax your leg muscles. Your partner will tap you if you are not breathing or if you tense your body.

It doesn't matter how aroused you become. Tell your partner your level every few minutes, whether the level is higher or lower than the one before. Keep your focus on the point of contact between your skin and your partner's skin. Relax your body completely and focus on your partner's touch. Don't move your body. If you approach orgasm, just passively let it happen. This way you will become familiar with all of the body sensations that happen as you approach orgasm and when you have an orgasm.

If you are a woman who has difficulty reaching orgasm, *allow yourself to relax* when you are passive during the arousal monitoring exercise. It doesn't matter whether you lubricate or not, or how high you go on your scale of arousal. Just let your partner know what you feel. Try not to move around, because tensing and moving at this stage will not make your arousal stronger, it will only make your arousal level go down. Taking a few deep breaths and relaxing your muscles will allow your body to experience more sexual arousal. Experience your entire sexual response cycle without interference from your brain. Get used to how you feel at the different levels of arousal.

If you have vaginismus, experience this exercise as you would another genital caress. Practice relaxing and distinguishing your levels of arousal. You may not have had previous experiences with this much arousal. Enjoy the feelings and begin to get used to them.

Sequence for Arousal Monitoring
Focusing caress — First person — 10 minutes
Focusing caress — Second person — 10 minutes
Front and genital caress — woman active — 10 minutes
Arousal monitoring — man active — 15 to 20 minutes
Feedback

Peaking

Men, so far you have done nondemand oral sex and genital caressing. If your partner has remained relaxed and passive, she may have already gone through her entire sexual response cycle to orgasm. Now I will share a few techniques you can do for your pleasure (they are very sensuous), but which will also be very stimulating for your partner. Remember, the more *you* enjoy yourself and focus on what you do, the more she will feel free to enjoy herself.

Begin with focusing caresses. Then the woman may do a nondemand front and genital caress with the man. The woman then lies comfortably on her back. She should breathe evenly and relax her muscles. The following instructions are for the male partner.

Begin a nondemand front caress. Caress the genital area with some baby oil, moving as *slowly* as possible. Gently spread your partner's legs so that you can see her inner vaginal lips. *Slowly* begin to use your tongue. Let her legs lie relaxed—don't prop them up. *Slowly* lick from the bottom of the vaginal opening up the center of the lips with the tip of your tongue. You will feel your tongue go over her clitoris (as if it were a "speed bump"). Repeat several times, each time *more slowly*. If your partner is very relaxed and remains passive, she may feel reflex leg spasms and possibly orgasm.

Next, insert the tip of one of your fingers into the vagina and play with the muscles around the vaginal opening. Feel the PC muscle spasm as it tightens around your finger. There are many sensitive nerve endings in the outer third of the vagina. Slowly move just the tip of your finger back and forth through the opening.

Women, focus intensely on these movements as your partner does them. You will also be peaking. Tell your partner when you reach a "3" or "4" level of arousal. He will then caress another area of your body until your arousal decreases one or two levels. Then peak up to level "5," "6," "7," "8," "9," and "10" if possible.

Choose the levels at which you would like to peak. Don't worry if you don't go all the way the first time you do the exercise. The important thing is not how aroused you become, but whether you are able to focus, breathe, and relax your leg muscles. Also, remember that the sensations involved with the downcurve of the peak are as important to recognize as the sensations involved with the upcurve.

The man should remember to focus, relax, and move slowly enough that he helps the woman build to each peak slowly. Repeat this exercise until you can do four or five peaks of about five minutes per peak. Fifteen or twenty minutes of peaking will intensify your orgasm.

Sequence for Peaking
Focusing caress — First person — 10 minutes
Focusing caress — Second person — 10 minutes
Front and genital caress — woman active — 10 minutes
Peaking — man active with hand and oral —
15 to 20 minutes
Feedback

Vaginal Peaking—Man Active

In the first vaginal peaking session the man will be active. Do the initial steps as described in the preceding exercise—focusing caresses, front caresses, and genital caresses. After the woman has peaked twice (around "5" or "6") with hand and oral stimulation, she bends her legs and raises them in the air. The man then kneels in the trident position. Remember that this position puts the man's center of gravity in his pelvis and legs rather than in his arms and chest.

The man *slowly* rubs his penis up along the vaginal lips, the same way he did with his tongue in the previous exercise. Feel the clitoris as a "bump" that you slowly cross with your penis. The woman should peak once with this type of slow stimulation. Both partners should continue to focus, breathe deeply, and relax their leg muscles. When the woman's arousal has decreased one or two levels, the man inserts his penis and *slowly* begins to thrust.

Men, tease your partner with your penis. Insert it only an inch or so and tease her PC muscle with it a few times. Then slowly move it all the way in and all the way out of the vagina. Move in a circular motion rather than just straight in and out. Move as slowly as you can. Continue to focus, breathe, and relax.

Slowly caress the inside of the vagina with the penis. Think of your penis as a giant tongue which is licking the inside of the vagina. Feel the walls along the sides and along the bottom of the vagina. Remember to move as slowly as you can, feeling every millimeter of skin on your penis and in your partner's vagina. If your penis has a curve to it, see if you can feel the G spot. Move your penis all the way in until you reach the area beyond the cervix. Squeeze your PC muscle and hold it. Either G spot or cul-de-sac stimulation may result in orgasm for the woman.

Women, allow your partner to support your legs so that you can relax them. Breathe deeply when you feel your arousal build. Tell your partner when you reach a peak (try "6," "7," "8," and "9" if possible). Your partner will slow down or stop to allow your arousal to go down. If you feel orgasm approaching, allow it to happen by focusing, breathing, and relaxing your leg muscles.

If you do not have an orgasm in this exercise, do not worry about it. Do not try to work at having one by moving or tensing. Enjoy whatever level of arousal you reach. After four or five peaks, ask your partner if he wants to ejaculate, then end the exercise.

Sequence for Vaginal Peaking With the Man Active
Focusing caress — First person — 10 minutes
Focusing caress — Second person — 10 minutes
Front and genital caress — woman active — 10 minutes
Vaginal peaking — man active — 20 to 30 minutes
Feedback

❤

How enjoyable you find this vaginal peaking exercise depends to a great extent on how slowly the man moves during the whole exercise. He should take his time with a front caress and manual and oral peaking prior to the vaginal peaking.

You may want to repeat the vaginal peaking exercise several times. I have described many different ways that the man can move and he may want to practice them for several sessions until they become comfortable and enjoyable for him. It may be too confusing or distracting to try to practice everything in one session.

Vaginal Peaking—Woman Active

Now that you have practiced vaginal peaking with the man active, we will switch control of the exercise to the woman. Women, begin with focusing caresses. Then do a genital caress or oral sex with your partner. Remember to take pleasure for yourself and focus on everything you do. By now you should be able to tell whether you are relaxed and how aroused you are.

When your partner has an erection, *slowly* sit on it. Kneel on top of him and slowly move up and down. Your partner should remain relaxed and passive.

There are a number of ways for a woman to thrust. You can kneel so that you move straight up and down on the penis. This provides one type of stimulation. Use long thrusts and allow the penis to go all the way in and all the way out. Or you can squat over your partner if you have strong leg muscles. You can rest part of your weight on the palms of your hands and use your arm strength to move yourself up and down on the penis. This position will also produce a vertical movement.

Perhaps the most sensuous way to do this is to change your position slightly so that while you are still on top, you are thrusting back and forth on the penis rather than up and down. Kneel over your partner and lay against his chest. Support yourself on your elbows, and keep your buttocks as high in the air as possible while still keeping the penis inside of you. This will put the penis in contact with your G spot. You will be able to feel your partner's penis rubbing against the G spot as you slowly thrust back and forth.

Do pelvic thrusts. Think of yourself as thrusting

your buttocks *up* along the penis rather than down on it. Move your hips in a circular motion and slowly thrust the penis all the way in and almost all the way out. Focus on every millimeter of the penile head and shaft as it goes in and out. Swivel your pelvis so that you can create more sensations along the shaft of the penis. Feel the contact with the G spot and along the sides of the vagina. Go as slowly as possible and think of your vagina as a mouth that is sucking your partner's penis.

Peak to "6," "7," "8," and "9," or peak several times at "9." At the moment before orgasm, open your eyes, take a deep breath, and stop thrusting. Passively experience your orgasm—allow it to happen without moving. Feel your PC muscle spasm around the penis. You will feel your orgasm as a shivering or spasming which may include not only your PC muscle, but your arms, legs, and facial muscles.

In another variation, practice using your PC muscle to increase your sensations during intercourse. Wait until you are extremely aroused ("9" plus) before you squeeze your PC muscle. This may also trigger an orgasm. You can also practice using the cul-de-sac and the area around the cervix as sites for stimulation.

❤

It is also possible to learn to have an orgasm immediately upon penetration. Begin this peaking session with focusing caresses (such as back caresses) by each partner. Then the man lies on his back. The woman may do a front caress, genital caress, or nondemand oral sex for her own pleasure—whatever she likes and whatever is easiest for her to focus on. By this time, the man should be experienced with focusing, breathing, and relaxing. He remains passive during this exercise.

When the man becomes erect, kneel over him and use his penis to pleasure yourself. Masturbate with his penis. Remember to breathe, and keep your leg muscles as relaxed as is possible in this position. Use your partner's penis to slowly peak yourself up to high levels including "6," "7," "8," and "9" if possible.

If you start to feel anxious, you know what to do—focus and/or back up to a previous part of the exercise with which you were comfortable (for example, the genital caress). Peak up to "9" by *slowly* rubbing the penis on the clitoris and the outside of the vagina. Masturbate with the penis rather than touching your clitoris with your fingers. Keep your eyes closed. Then when you are on the brink of orgasm ("9" plus), open your eyes, take a deep breath, and thrust yourself all the way down on the penis. It is likely you will have an orgasm.

The secret to being able to do this is the peaking process, not the penetration itself. You may need to spend fifteen or twenty minutes using your partner's penis to peak yourself up. Don't forget to allow your arousal to decrease somewhat between peaks. While caressing your partner and masturbating with his penis, it is important to focus on exactly what you are doing and stay in the here and now. If you anticipate the orgasm or worry about it, it won't happen. Your ability to concentrate, peak yourself up to "9," and totally focus on that "9" state of arousal is what will produce the orgasm upon penetration.

Another variation is to peak yourself up to "9" several times (rather than only once) and then sit on the penis. Whichever way you decide will be best for you (of course, you could always do both), it is likely that this exercise will show you and your partner that you don't need long sessions of intercourse in order to reach orgasm.

You will probably want to repeat these exercises several times, varying the type of stimulation. The man may gradually add in more and more movement. One variation is for the woman to sit on the penis and thrust as slowly as she can. The man then thrusts back at the same speed. The woman is in charge of speeding up the thrusting or slowing it down, and the man follows. Both partners focus on the exact point of contact between their bodies.

The focus of the exercise can also be reversed, with the man slowly beginning the motion and the woman following. Making the exercise sensual depends on *how well the partners focus together,* rather than the speed of the thrusting. The partners should look at each other as they thrust. If you are focused on your own feelings, you should also have a sense of how close your partner is to orgasm. If you are moving and focusing together, it is likely that your levels of arousal will be parallel.

The first partner to reach level "9" should signal this, perhaps by opening the eyes wide or saying the partner's name. The other partner can then speed up the motion so that both reach orgasm at the same time. As you reach orgasm, take a deep breath, relax your leg muscles, open your eyes and look at your partner.

Sequence for Vaginal Peaking With the Woman Active
Focusing caress — First person — 10 minutes
Focusing caress — Second person — 10 minutes
Vaginal Peaking — woman active — 20 to 30 minutes
Feedback

Plateauing

A woman can plateau—maintain herself at a certain level of arousal—either when she is active or passive. For example, the woman may lie on her back and her partner may caress her genitals with his hand. When she reaches a certain pleasant level of arousal (say "7"), she should tell her partner to stop caressing. He should stop until her arousal level decreases to "6½," and he should then caress until she asks him to stop at "7½." Repeat this stop-and-start procedure several times. You can plateau at any level you like, but it is especially enjoyable to plateau at a high level. Your partner can stimulate you either manually or orally.

Sequence for Plateauing
Focusing caress — First person — 10 minutes
Focusing caress — Second person — 10 minutes
Plateauing — man active — manual or oral
— 15 to 20 minutes
Feedback

❤

A woman can also plateau during intercourse, with either the man or the woman active. If you would like the man to be active, use the position described under vaginal peaking, with the woman on her back with her legs bent and in the air. The man then kneels in front of her and begins to stroke her vaginal lips with his penis. Both partners should remember to focus, breathe, and relax, as always.

The man inserts his penis and *slowly* begins to stroke. The woman then tells him when she reaches a plateau level at which she would like to remain. Tell him to stop and start so that you maintain yourself at that level for several minutes.

You can plateau at any level you like. It is easiest to practice at the lower levels, and this will help you have more enjoyment when you are ready to try plateauing at the higher levels. Try to plateau at "9" for as long as you can and then let yourself fall over the edge into an orgasm.

Also practice plateauing during intercourse when you are active. The man should lie on his back while you stimulate yourself using his penis. You then climb on his penis and plateau by thrusting and stopping or slowing down.

Sequences for Vaginal Plateauing
Focusing caress — First person — 10 minutes
Focusing caress — Second person — 10 minutes
Genital caress — woman active — 10 minutes
Vaginal Plateauing — man active — 15 to 20 minutes
Feedback

Focusing caress — First person — 10 minutes
Focusing caress — Second person — 10 minutes
Genital caress — woman active — 10 minutes
Vaginal Plateauing — woman active — 15 to 20 minutes
Feedback

The exercises in this chapter will help you to reach and sustain high levels of arousal. Learning to plateau at "9" can also help you have multiple orgasms. After one orgasm, have your partner stimulate you again before your arousal decreases below "9." At that point it may only take a few strokes to push you over the edge to orgasm again.

Chapter 13

❤

Exercises for
Inhibited Ejaculation

An inhibited ejaculation problem is defined not so much by the lack of ability to ejaculate as it is by the man's feelings about the situation. Psychologically-based inhibited ejaculation usually involves the feeling of "working at" ejaculating rather than enjoying the sensations of intercourse. Frequently, the cause of frustration for the man is the fact that he is working at it, rather than the inability to ejaculate itself.

There may be a sensation that the physical charge or arousal has remained high during intercourse, but that the emotional arousal has remained at or backed down to a low level. Inhibited ejaculation is this feeling of high physical arousal coupled with the inability to feel close to ejaculation.

Most men with an inhibited ejaculation problem are able to ejaculate with masturbation if they want to, but are not able to ejaculate within the vagina during inter-course. The problem may even involve the ability to ejaculate during intercourse with a particular woman but not with other women. Like other sexual problems, in-hibited ejaculation is a problem which usually builds up gradually. As the man experiences the inability to ejacu-late more and more often, and withdraws to masturbate outside the vagina, the problem becomes worse. He needs to reverse the process and move closer and closer to ejaculating in the vagina rather than farther and farther away from it.

A short-term case of inhibited ejaculation, where the problem has occurred for less than a year, can be treated quickly with sex therapy techniques, and will respond extremely well to the exercises described in this chapter. In fact, chances are that if you had a short-term case of inhibited ejaculation, the basic sensate focus exercises helped you significantly.

A long-standing case of inhibited ejaculation, how-ever, can be one of the most difficult sexual problems to deal with, and it often takes a long time (sometimes years) for the man to relearn to ejaculate in the vagina. It is particularly difficult to heal a problem that has been going on for a long time (twenty years or more) and is fueled by anger toward women in general or toward a specific female partner. This anger may not be on a conscious level. When I work with men with this type of problem, I often see that the anger has become such a part of their personality that they are unaware of it; indeed, most of them would deny that they are angry at their partners, and insist that they like women and they like sexual activity.

If you are unable to ejaculate because of repressed anger you may still be able to learn to ejaculate through the exercises described in this book, as the exercises are quite powerful. The healthiest way to deal with long-standing anger, however, would be to work on the underlying issues with a competent therapist.

The anger you are holding inside may be overcome to some degree by fostering intimacy in your relationship, and you can do that by doing the exercises described in this chapter. In order for this to work, you will have to *want* it to work—you can't do these exercises halfway, as they will definitely produce a certain amount of intimacy. If you know that you do not want that intimacy, then do not attempt these exercises.

There are a couple of things you should stop doing before you begin to deal with your inhibited ejaculation problem. First, you should limit the amount of time you spend having intercourse. For example, if you find you are having intercourse for half an hour and are not able to ejaculate even though you want to and are trying to, then limit yourself to a certain time frame. Tell your partner that from now on you will stop at ten minutes or fifteen minutes or some other mutually agreed upon comfortable limit, whether you have ejaculated or not. Contrary to what you may believe, it will not hurt you to become aroused and then naturally allow the arousal to go down without ejaculating.

Limiting the time you spend in intercourse will allow you to stop thinking, "If only I had another few seconds, few minutes, or half hour, I know I could ejaculate." If you are the partner of a man who is having problems with inhibited ejaculation, there is no need to feel guilty about ending intercourse before he ejaculates. Prolonging intercourse will not help inhibited ejaculation. Doing more of what you are already doing will not help, whereas learning some new activities will.

Limiting the time you spend in intercourse will also force you to focus on the intercourse sensations that are happening in the here and now, rather than on those that may happen in the future. It will also force you to admit that you have a problem ejaculating, which is something that you may not have really accepted.

Also, resolve that from now on when you have intercourse, you will do it as slowly as possible, and in a sensate focus, nondemand fashion. You have probably become used to a hard-driving mode of intercourse which is actually making your problem worse. When you catch yourself going too fast, consciously make an effort to slow down.

Sensuous Kissing

In the first exercise to foster intimacy, you and your partner will take turns kissing each other on the mouth. The active person should kiss as if it were a caress. Caress the outside and inside of your partner's mouth with your tongue. Focus, breathe, and relax, just as with any sensate focus exercise.

Each partner should do the kissing caress for at least five to ten minutes. Stop occasionally and gaze into each other's eyes. Finish the kissing caress with five or ten minutes of mutual kissing.

The goal of this exercise is not to leave each other's lips and tongues sore. The idea is rather to kiss as slowly, softly, seriously, sensuously, and intimately as possible. If you find you are going too fast, kissing too hard, or are unable to maintain concentration, stop for a moment, focus your attention, and start over more slowly.

It is important that you do this exercise separately from any other exercise *at least once.* Talk about your feelings about the exercise after you do it. Then, use this kissing exercise as a prelude to the other exercises in this chapter.

If you feel anxious during this exercise, the reason for your discomfort is that this exercise promotes tremendous intimacy between partners, whether you want it to or not. Remember, if you feel anxious or uncomfortable during the exercise, do what you would do if you felt anxious during any exercise—tell your partner you are anxious and back up to something you are comfortable with. For example, if you are uncomfortable looking into your partner's eyes, practice the exercise with your eyes closed until you are more comfortable. Then move to the more intimate version of the exercise and repeat it as many times as you need to until you are completely comfortable with it.

The Importance of Self-Caressing

In order to deal with inhibited ejaculation, you need to "overlearn" the genital self-caress and self-peaking exercises described in the chapter on exercises to do by yourself. Set aside separate times for having time-limited intercourse with your partner and for doing the genital self-caress. You may do a genital caress as often as every day, but allow yourself to go all the way to ejaculation only if you can do it without "working at it." During the exercises you do by yourself, train yourself to become aroused with a gentle touch to your penis, rather than the fast or vigorous motions you may previously have masturbated with.

During the first phase of dealing with inhibited ejaculation, keep intercourse and "working on the problem" completely separate. During intercourse with your partner, agree on a time frame and concentrate only on the feelings of pleasure. During the genital self-caress, overpractice the "9" level of arousal—do several peaks at level "9" so that you become highly familiar with the sensations of arousal that accompany that "9" feeling. Remember to breathe and keep your leg muscles as relaxed as possible. Then practice allowing yourself to fall over the edge into ejaculation, rather than working at ejaculation. Do this by relaxing your leg muscles and taking a deep breath at the point of ejaculation.

As you do the genital self-caress, maintain awareness of both your physical response level (the hardness of your erection) and your emotional response level (how close you feel to ejaculation). Any time your emotional charge drops below your physical charge, slow down and focus until they are in step. If you need to let your erection go down in order to connect your physical and emotional charge, that is fine. Practice caressing yourself in such a way that the two charge levels stay together.

After you have practiced the self-caressing, go through the basic sensate focus exercises and the peaking process with a partner as described for premature ejaculation problems. It is very important for you to learn to peak, so that you begin to get a sense of how emotionally aroused you are when you are with your partner. Then go through the exercises for female arousal. You and your partner will both enjoy them, and focusing your activities on your partner's arousal for a few exercises will prevent you from "working too hard" at trying to ejaculate. If you have experienced the peaking process and still find you need to withdraw from the vagina in order to ejaculate, try the following progression of exercises.

Intercourse with Masturbation

Begin each session with a focusing caress. This can be either the back, face, or foot caress. Remember the sensate focus principles: Focus, breathe, and relax. Move on to a few minutes of mutual sensuous kissing.

Then lie passively on your back. Your partner should do a genital caress and vaginal peaking up to level "9" if possible. At "9," she should withdraw your penis from her vagina and let you masturbate to ejaculation.

Masturbate without tensing your legs—use pelvic

rolls instead, if you want to move. Remember to breathe as you feel yourself getting aroused. If you tend to masturbate with fast strokes, try to slow down and touch yourself in as sensuous a manner as possible. Have your partner also put her hand on your penis while you masturbate.

The next time you have intercourse, alternate the intercourse with masturbation at high arousal levels. Peak up to level "8" during intercourse, withdraw and masturbate, then reinsert and do another peak. Do three or four combination intercourse and masturbation peaks, and then ejaculate with masturbation.

The next time you and your partner do an exercise, alternate intercourse and masturbation at high levels again. Then ejaculate into your partner's vagina.

If you usually go into another room to masturbate, you may first need to practice doing it in the same room with your partner. Have her shut her eyes at first if you are uncomfortable with her watching. Ejaculate either on yourself or on your partner if she agrees. Don't forget to give feedback to each other after the exercise. If you are able to masturbate to ejaculation with your partner watching, there is an excellent chance that you will be able to relearn to ejaculate inside the vagina.

Do not pressure your partner to go faster during intercourse. Allow your partner to caress or have intercourse at her own speed. Breathe and keep your leg muscles relaxed. Focus on the feelings as your partner caresses your genitals or moves up and down on top of you. Don't work at ejaculating if you feel you are getting close.

You may have gotten into a habit of anticipating the ejaculation before you are close, and then working at it. Use the arousal monitoring, peaking, and intercourse exercises to learn what those high levels of arousal feel like again. Nothing bad will happen to you if you passively become very aroused and then allow the arousal to decrease naturally without ejaculating. What results in negative feelings is working at ejaculating and then not being able to ejaculate because you are working at it.

If you are the partner of a man with inhibited ejaculation, go as slowly as you can during the genital caresses. Don't allow yourself to be pressured into moving faster than is comfortable for you. Continue the nondemand caressing. If your partner pressures you, back up to a previous nongenital exercise for a while.

Sequence for Intercourse with Masturbation
Focusing caress — First person — 10 minutes
Focusing caress — Second person — 10 minutes
Genital caress and vaginal peaking — woman active
— 15 to 20 minutes
Masturbation — 1 to 10 minutes
Feedback

Sequence for Alternating Intercourse and Masturbation
Focusing caress — First person — 10 minutes
Focusing caress — Second person — 10 minutes
Intercourse with masturbation — man active
— 15 to 30 minutes
Feedback

If the intercourse with masturbation strategy does not result in ejaculation, there are a number of other ways you can approach the problem. Think of these exercises as pleasure, not work. Your problem has been that you feel that ejaculating is something you have to *try* to do. You need to relax, so that your body can produce its ejaculation response naturally.

You should follow the principle called "shaping" or "successive approximations of behavior." Choose exercises to take you closer and closer (both physically and emotionally) to ejaculating inside the vagina. Try to determine the *exact* point where your sexual response is shutting down—the exact point where you lose your sensate focus and start *trying* to ejaculate. Your partner may be able to help you recognize this point, because she may be able to tell when you switch from enjoying yourself to working at ejaculating.

After you have been able to recognize that point, you need to overpractice your response right before that point. For example, if the point when you start trying or working at it is when you feel yourself get to level "8" inside the vagina, you need to do several exercises (complete with focusing caresses and feedback) in which you bring yourself up to "8" and maintain level "8" by plateauing.

I describe below a typical progression of exercises, all of which can also be done separately, with focusing caresses beforehand and mutual feedback afterwards. The reason that inhibited ejaculation can take so long to deal with is that the best approach for you may be to do each of these steps as a separate exercise.

This sequence of exercises has worked for a number of my clients with inhibited ejaculation. Remember to focus, breathe, and relax throughout each exercise.

1. Masturbate to ejaculation with your partner in the room.

2. Masturbate to ejaculation with your partner on the bed next to you watching.

3. Masturbate to ejaculation and ejaculate on your partner's stomach.

4. Masturbate to ejaculation and ejaculate at the entrance to your partner's vagina.

5. Masturbate to ejaculation while on your back and signal your partner to climb on top *as you are ejaculating* (not before). By now you are probably able to know that you are going to ejaculate a few seconds before it happens. Part of your problem before was that you anticipated it too soon.

6. Masturbate to ejaculation while kneeling in front of your partner and thrust into the vagina as you ejaculate. Continue to have intercourse in a slow, focused manner until your erection goes down.

7. Masturbate, peak, and penetrate at an arousal level of "9." Keep your hand on your penis as you thrust in and out of the vagina, and ejaculate into the vagina.

8. Masturbate while you have intercourse and take your hand off your penis as you ejaculate. Practice this several times, removing your hand from your penis earlier and earlier.

❤

Any time you are having intercourse, remember to keep your thigh muscles as relaxed as possible and thrust by using pelvic rolls. During intercourse, any time you feel your emotional charge drop below your physical charge, stop for a moment and allow the two sensations to merge (even if your erection goes down a level or two).

Whenever you do a sensate focus exercise by yourself or with your partner, you also need to be aware of your PC muscle. Many men with inhibited ejaculation problems consciously or unconsciously tense their PC muscle as they reach high levels of arousal. (We have already seen in the chapter on erections how tensing your PC muscle at low levels of arousal can cause erection problems.) Tensing your PC muscle at high arousal levels can cause an inability to ejaculate.

In order to break this habit, you may need to do several sensate focus exercises (genital caresses or intercourse) in which you become aware of the condition of your PC muscle and consciously relax it. It is especially important that you relax the area of the PC group associated with the anal sphincter.

Dealing with inhibited ejaculation can be a time-consuming process, and may become frustrating for both partners. That is why it is important to increase intimacy at the same time as you work through the exercises. Kissing is one way to do this, and another is the mutual eye gaze. Don't be afraid to tell each other if you feel angry or frustrated. It is possible to talk about these issues without blaming the other person and, in fact, sharing feelings about the process is the best way for you and your partner to become more intimate.

Chapter 14

❤

Exercises to Reduce Performance Pressure

The exercises in this chapter can be used any time after you have completed the basic sensate focus exercises (the face, back, front, and genital caresses). You may still be experiencing feelings of performance pressure even though most of the time you are able to focus, breathe, and relax. If you are dealing with a specific sexual problem, you may reach a point when you feel you are working too hard and trying to get better. These exercises can relieve some of the strain, and the new approach may help you make a breakthrough. They can either be done exactly as described, or you can make them into a complete session with focusing caresses first and feedback afterwards.

Towel Over the Face

This exercise is especially good for women who have

problems reaching orgasm and men who have problems with erections. Often these problems are due in part to worrying about what the partner thinks about you. Searching our partner's facial expression for an indication of his or her response or feelings can distract us from our own enjoyment of the sexual exchange. Covering the partner's face removes a source of feedback and pressure about our "performance." This exercise can be done with either partner active or passive. Use this exercise if either partner still feels, "I can't really enjoy myself unless my partner is also pleased."

To begin, the man lies on his back with a towel or a piece of clothing placed loosely over his face. Women, you are to pretend that your partner's body is a toy that you will be allowed to play with for twenty minutes or half an hour. (If you do something that really bothers your partner, he will let you know, as in previous exercises.) You can use any part of your partner's body in order to give yourself maximum enjoyment.

Here are some suggestions. Slowly rub yourself all over your partner. Lick his body. Masturbate with his penis. Climb on top of his penis and slowly thrust in and out if you have reached that point in the program. Experiment with different angles for thrusting. Masturbate by rubbing your clitoris on your partner's knees or hips. Use your partner's penis to find your G spot. You may want to get out of yourself for a few minutes by pretending that you are someone else. You may do anything but work at having an orgasm.

Men, when you are passive, you are not to move or respond in any way. That means no talking, no moaning, no twitching, even if your partner drives you crazy. Just focus on what she does. If you become aroused, if you have an erection, or if you have an orgasm, just enjoy yourself. Your partner has been instructed to enjoy herself with whatever is available on your body. Do not push any arousal away, and do not try to make it better.

Besides reducing performance pressure by eliminating facial feedback, this exercise allows you to abdicate all responsibility for the interaction; when you are passive, the only possible thing you can do is relax and enjoy. Your partner is completely responsible for what happens—you do not have to respond at all.

Doing this exercise with the man passive and the woman active is helpful for men with erection problems and for women who have problems reaching orgasm. Reversing the roles can benefit men with inhibited ejaculation problems and women who try too hard to reach orgasm. You will probably want to try out both roles in this exercise.

Some people react strongly to this exercise. If you are used to having sex a certain way (for example, if the man is always the initiator), the woman's activity may cause the man acute discomfort. It is not unusual for clients to be unable to do this exercise at first. When in the active role, they stall out and do nothing, or they drive themselves crazy trying to force their partner to respond. In the passive role, they go crazy because they *want* to respond. They think, "How can she really be enjoying herself if I'm not doing anything?"

For other people, not being able to see their partner's facial reactions is frustrating, or feels unnatural. But with practice, this exercise can become extremely pleasurable. It is a relief to be able to enjoy yourself without having to do anything. I think all of us like the feeling of being "done to" once in a while.

The towel over the face exercise can reinforce the idea that you are responsible for your own arousal. It can encourage you to experiment with sexual activities you may not have done before because someone was watching. It can force you to pay attention to your own enjoyment because there is nothing else to pay attention to. It can wean you from depending on your partner's response for your enjoyment.

This exercise can also reduce some of your inhibitions about being "animalistic" during sexual activity. Sexual activity serves a number of purposes, one of which is to express love for your partner. There are other legitimate reasons for having sexual activity, and one is to express the fact that sexual activity is also an animal activity. Feel free to growl, grunt, or bare your teeth as you touch and squeeze parts of your partner's body.

In another version of this exercise, the active person also wears some sort of a blindfold. This forces the active person as well to focus completely on sensations.

Sequence for the Towel Over the Face Exercise
Focusing caress — First person — 10 minutes
Focusing caress — Second person — 10 minutes
Towel — Person #1 — 15 minutes
Towel — Person #2 — 15 minutes
Feedback

Ask for What You Want

This exercise begins the minute you enter the room—you do not do focusing caresses to prepare for it. The partner who is active asks for anything that he or she wants. Let's assume that the woman is active first. Nothing will happen in the exercise until she requests it. If she wants her partner to remove his clothes, she must say, "Take off your clothes."

When you are active, you need to tell your partner everything that you want him or her to do. You may ask for anything that you can think of that you would like your partner to do, but you need to be specific. If what he does is not *exactly* what you wanted, say so and give him directions until he gets it right. Feel free to enjoy whatever you have told your partner to do for as long as you want to. When active, you may also *do* whatever you like, as long as you tell your partner what you are going to do. For example, if you would like to be active for a while, you could say, "I want you to lie back so I can caress you for a while."

If you are the passive partner, do as your partner asks. You will have your turn later. Refuse only if your partner asks you to do something that you consider painful or unpleasant. Much as you might want to initiate something, don't—unless your partner requests it. See if you can actually do what your partner asks you to, but do it for your own enjoyment and focus on it. The secret is to accommodate your partner's wishes while still doing the activities for yourself.

This exercise can sometimes become awkward because many people are not used to asking for what they want. Sometimes a client and I have just sat and looked at each other for several minutes because he couldn't think of anything to ask for or was afraid to ask for anything.

When you are the "asker," be assertive and don't settle for something that is not really what you wanted. When you are the "askee," accommodate your partner but do everything for your own pleasure as much as possible by focusing on your own sensual enjoyment.

Make your requests clear. For example, instead of saying, "Would you like to give me a front caress?" say, "Give me a front caress," "Please give me a front caress," or "I want you to give me a front caress." If you do not want to do something your partner asks, just say "No." If your partner says no to some activity, it doesn't mean "No, never, that's disgusting." It simply means "No, I do not want to do that particular activity right now."

You can do this exercise with each person being in

the active role for half an hour. The exercise can be stressful, but it can also pinpoint problems you may be having in asserting or enjoying yourself. After the exercise, talk about how you felt. Tell your partner if you had trouble knowing what you wanted, asking, or enjoying. Tell your partner if you had thoughts such as, "I would have asked for such-and-such, but I was afraid you wouldn't do it."

Your anxiety level during this exercise can give you real insight into whether you are still uncomfortable with accepting pleasure for yourself. If you are uncomfortable, practice asking for one or two small things during each session until you are more comfortable.

Besides making you more comfortable with asserting yourself sexually, the ask-for-what-you-want exercise can help you feel a sense of equity in your relationship. If you do the exercise the way I have described, each partner has an equal chance to ask and to give.

Sequence for the Ask for What You Want Exercise
Asking — First person — 30 minutes
Asking — Second person — 30 minutes
Feedback

The Zombie

The zombie (also known as "the slave") is a more extreme version of the ask-for-what-you-want exercise, in which one partner is in control throughout the session. One partner orders the other around for a half hour or an hour, and the "zombie" partner is required to do anything sexual the other partner asks (unless there is a severe objection to it). The zombie literally acts like a zombie—silent, obedient, and unresponsive.

The zombie exercise is a way to experiment with loss of control. Some of your sexual problems may stem from your feeling that you have to be in control of your body or your sexual responses. A few minutes as the zombie may convince you that while you do not want to be out of control all the time, temporarily relinquishing some control of your body is not that bad. It can even be a relief not to have to be responsible for anything that happens.

The zombie exercise is extreme and should only be done if you are comfortable with the idea. If done at the right time, it can build trust between partners. You may also find out some things about yourself that you didn't know. You may find that you are actually comfortable being totally in control or totally out of control. The zombie exercise is a safe way to explore these feelings. Being the zombie with a person you trust is in a sense the ultimate in performance pressure. Can you deal with it? At the very least, you will find out if it is something you truly dislike.

This exercise is not an excuse to be sadistic or shock your partner. It is a way to build trust and to practice dealing with extreme performance pressure. When you are the zombie, do you try to perform or wonder if you are doing things right? Or are you so well trained in sensate focus that you are able to move into the sensate focus mode right away and *enjoy* the interaction? If you become performance-oriented during the zombie exercise, it will literally show you "how not to feel" during other sensate focus exercises.

Sequence for the Zombie Exercise
Zombie — 30 to 60 minutes
Feedback

Switch Focus

There are a number of things you can focus on during sexual activity. The switch focus exercise will help you tune your sensate focus abilities. Begin with focusing caresses, then lie in a comfortable side by side position in which you can touch each other's genitals with one hand. Caress each other's genitals simultaneously throughout the exercise.

When you begin the mutual caress, both of you should focus on the man's genitals. Then after several minutes, switch your focus to the woman's genitals. For the next switch, concentrate on the man's hand. For the last switch, focus on the woman's hand. Remember to breath and relax also.

This exercise is not easy! In fact, it is about as hard to do as it is to describe. It takes concentration and self-discipline to focus on all of these different perspectives. One person should be in charge of deciding when to switch the focus, and should say out loud, "Now, let's both focus on your genitals," for example.

The switch focus exercise can benefit men with erection and inhibited ejaculation problems and women who have trouble becoming aroused and reaching orgasm. Ideally, this exercise will occupy your mind so completely that you will forget about erections and arousal and just focus on feelings.

The switch focus exercise can be done with oral sex also. Practice switching your focus to your tongue, your partner's genitals, your partner's tongue, and your genitals.

In another version of this exercise, switch back and forth between focusing on what feels good for you and focusing on trying to please your partner. Use this version of the exercise if it is difficult for you to rid yourself of that last vestige of worry about your partner's response. Notice the difference in feelings when you are passive if your partner tries to please you, versus if your partner focuses on enjoying. This exercise should convince you that if you do what feels good for you, your partner can't help but enjoy it.

Sequence for the Switch Focus Exercise
Focusing caress — First person — 10 minutes
Focusing caress — Second person — 10 minutes
Switch focus — 20 minutes
Feedback

Mutual Masturbation

In this exercise, the partners take turns masturbating with the other watching. Or you may both lie together and masturbate at the same time.

If you take turns masturbating, this exercise can help you act out any exhibitionist fantasies you have. It will also show you how your partner likes to be touched. You don't have to masturbate all the way to orgasm. Use vibrators or other sexual aids if you like. You could also share one of your sexual fantasies with your partner while you masturbate.

If you would like to masturbate at the same time, lie together on the bed. In one version of this exercise, you can stimulate yourself the way you would if you were alone. Ignore the fact that your partner is there. In another version, the partners may look at each other as they masturbate. This version of the exercise will build trust between partners.

Sequence for Mutual Masturbation Exercise
Focusing caress — First person — 10 minutes
Focusing caress — Second person — 10 minutes
Masturbation — First person — 15 minutes
Masturbation — Second person — 15 minutes
Feedback

or

Focusing caress — First person — 10 minutes
Focusing caress — Second person — 10 minutes
Masturbation — Both partners — 15 minutes
Feedback

Sensate Focus Intercourse

This is an exercise to use if you and your partner are a little burned out on doing exercises! It is a more advanced version of the nondemand penetration you learned in the chapter on peaking. A man who began the program with ejaculation or erection problems should use this exercise after he has attained some ejaculation control or is regularly having erections.

Begin the session with focusing caresses. Use whatever kind of stimulation you both like to prepare for intercourse. Decide on a position for intercourse in advance—use any position in which you are face to face.

The partner who is on top controls the speed of thrusting, and should start as *slowly* as possible. The other partner should follow at the same speed. Both partners are to focus intensely on the sensation of the penis in the vagina. Men, think of yourself as caressing the inside of your partner's vagina with your penis. Women, think of yourself as caressing your partner's penis with your vagina. Look at each other as you move. Relax and breathe.

Since you have already done peaking exercises with your partner, you will have a good idea of not only how aroused you are, but how aroused your partner is also. Follow your partner up to orgasm if you can. At the moment of orgasm, open your eyes wide and look into your partner's eyes.

❤

The exercises in this chapter are quite unusual and intense. You will need a strong foundation of trust and rapport with your partner in order to do them successfully. However, they have the potential to help you to make a real breakthrough if you are experiencing difficulty in reducing performance pressure.

Chapter 15

❤

Exercises for Breakthroughs

At some point in any program, certain sexual issues or problems seem to become especially stubborn. Nothing seems to help, or you feel burned out from "working" on the problem and wish for something different. The exercises in this chapter can be used if you reach an impasse where you just cannot seem to gain control of your ejaculation, have erections, or reach orgasm. They can also help to overcome any lingering problems with performance anxiety or spectatoring.

PC Squeeze

The PC squeeze exercise will help severe premature ejaculation problems that have not responded to the relaxation and awareness techniques described in the chapter on peaking. Before you take the time to learn the PC squeeze, though, try an easier option. Have your partner stimulate you to ejaculation at the *beginning* of a peaking session. If you ejaculate at the beginning of a session, you won't be worried about ejaculating during the peaking process. This will reduce your anxiety so that you will be able to learn how to peak. Once you have learned the peaking skills with your partner, you will no longer need to ejaculate at the beginning of a session.

If the above strategy does not work, you can learn the PC squeeze. Begin the session with focusing caresses. The man may then do a nondemand genital caress or oral sex if he desires.

The man lies on his back, remembering to focus, breathe, and relax all of his muscles. The woman then begins to caress his genitals as she would during a peaking exercise. When the man feels himself reach a low level of arousal (for example, a "4"), he squeezes his PC muscle several times until he feels his arousal go down. Repeat the exercise squeezing at "6," "7," "8," and "9" if possible. It goes without saying that before you can do this exercise, your PC muscle should be in good shape from the exercises you have been doing.

Squeezing your PC muscle in this way will probably cause your erection to go down at least part of the way, or you may actually trigger an ejaculation. This is nothing to worry about. Just wait a few minutes and start the exercise over.

It is possible to overdo the squeezing, and if you do this exercise for more than about half an hour you may temporarily find yourself unable to ejaculate at all. This is also nothing to worry about, as long as you are learning to recognize your levels of arousal and to temporarily decrease your arousal level by squeezing.

For the PC squeeze to control the ejaculation, you must be sure to squeeze only the PC muscle. You must make sure you are not tensing your abdomen, thigh, or buttocks muscles at the same time.

You may need to repeat this exercise a number of times until you become aware of how hard you need to squeeze in order to feel your arousal go down but have your erection stay up. When I teach the PC squeeze to clients, I tell them that they need to learn to "tap their brakes rather than slam on the brakes." After you have learned to do the squeeze with manual and oral stimulation, you can also practice it during intercourse. It is possible to squeeze your PC muscle at the moment of ejaculation, which I am told creates some unusually pleasurable sensations. A strong PC squeeze at the moment of orgasm can sometimes cause you to have an orgasm without the ejaculation. A few seconds later you could have another orgasm and ejaculate.

This exercise will show you that your ejaculations are under your control, which will help you relax. After you have mastered the PC squeeze so that you can allow yourself to relax, go on to the peaking exercises without the squeeze. Use the PC squeeze only as a tool to enable yourself to become comfortable enough so that you start learning to stay aroused through awareness and relaxation. Squeezing tends to reinforce the idea that you are "working" on your problem rather than relaxing and enjoying the stimulation. Squeezing should only be used for a few sessions and then you should return to the awareness and relaxation techniques, unless you want to experiment with the squeeze to see if you can have multiple orgasms.

Sequence for the PC Squeeze Exercise
Focusing caress — First person — 10 minutes
Focusing caress — Second person — 10 minutes
Genital caress — man active — 10 minutes
PC squeeze — woman active — hand and oral
— 15 to 20 minutes
Feedback

Sequence for Intercourse with PC Squeeze
Focusing caress — First person — 10 minutes
Focusing caress — Second person — 10 minutes
Intercourse with PC squeeze — 10 to 20 minutes

The Squeeze Technique

You may be familiar with the squeeze technique, which was recommended by Masters and Johnson and is used by most sex therapists. I usually teach the peaking process instead, but the squeeze technique is effective for some clients with very severe premature ejaculation problems.

Use the squeeze technique only if you have gone all the way through this program and are still not confident that you can control your ejaculations. Begin as you would any other session, with focusing caresses. The woman then caresses the man's penis while he is passive.

When the man reaches the state of arousal *right* before the point of ejaculatory inevitability, he signals the woman and she squeezes the head of his penis tightly between her thumb and first two fingers. After the woman squeezes his penis, the man will feel his arousal level decrease and his erection is likely to go down somewhat also.

You can repeat the squeeze several times in one session, after which the man should allow himself to ejaculate. You can also do the squeeze technique during intercourse, withdrawing the penis at high levels of arousal so the woman can squeeze it.

Breathe, relax, and focus on the sensations as you would during any other exercise. Again, use the squeeze technique only as a tool to bring yourself to the point where you are comfortable enough to begin peaking exercises without the squeeze.

Sequence for the Squeeze Technique
Focusing caress — First person — 10 minutes
Focusing caress — Second person — 10 minutes
Squeeze technique — woman active — 10 to 20 minutes
Feedback

Faking Orgasm

Faking orgasm in the way that I will describe here is very different from faking an orgasm to please your partner or because you think your partner expects you to have one. What you will learn here is to fake your body into thinking you are having an orgasm. This in turn can actually trigger the orgasm.

If you have passively experienced the peaking process and tried the female arousal techniques in this book, chances are good that you have had an orgasm (or several). However, if you have not experienced orgasm, try this exercise. This is most likely to help if you can successfully peak up to "9" but cannot seem to go over the edge.

Remember that the orgasmic response is a full body response, not something that only occurs in the genitals. At the moment of orgasm, your face contorts, your arms, legs, and neck spasm, and your PC muscle begins to contract. If you enact these body responses when you are at "9" plus, there is a chance that you will trigger the orgasm. The secret is to do them so that they feel good, and not in order to have the orgasm.

At "9" plus, take a deep breath, suck in your lower abdomen, hunch your shoulders into the bed, thrust your pelvis up, open your eyes wide, and relax your PC muscle. This may trigger the orgasm, which you will experience as a fluttering or spasming of the PC muscle.

Another way to do this is to wait until you are at the very brink of orgasm and then slam your PC muscle shut. This can often trigger the necessary spasms.

A third alternative is to pretend you are having an

orgasm and to act the way you think highly orgasmic women act. This is a more mental version of the exercise, which may involve moaning, contorting your face, or pretending that you are someone else. It can work best if what is holding you back is your image of yourself as someone who "doesn't do that sort of thing." Pretending that you are a highly arousable and orgasmic woman may allow you to practice orgasm techniques in a non-threatening way until you feel more comfortable with them.

All of these ways of triggering orgasm have several things in common. First, you have to be able to focus, breathe, and relax well enough to allow yourself to get up to level "9." You also have to be able to focus well enough so that you avoid having any distracting thoughts when you are at "9."

Use these orgasm techniques not as ends in themselves but as ways to accustom yourself to having orgasms. If you learn these triggers, soon you will be able to use them during intercourse. As with any skill that involves learning complex patterns of behavior and combining them, the first few tries will feel artificial. After you have practiced these techniques for a while, though, they will become habits and your relaxation at level "9" will trigger the orgasm.

A man with inhibited ejaculation can use the same techniques. Peak yourself up to level "9" either with masturbation, oral sex, or intercourse. When you are on the brink of orgasm, stop all movement, relax your pelvic muscles, take a deep breath, and open your eyes.

The secret of this technique is being able to reach an arousal level of "9" and not jump the gun. The first few times you try this, you may actually ejaculate without realizing it, because you are unfamiliar with the feeling. Try to build yourself up to "9" and just fall over the edge, rather than pushing yourself over. Plateauing at "9" can also be effective. Plateau for several minutes and then fool your body by increasing the stimulation when you would normally decrease it.

Sequence for Faking Orgasm
Focusing caress — First person — 10 minutes
Focusing caress — Second person — 10 minutes
Peaking or plateauing with practice of body orgasmic
response — 15 to 30 minutes

Stream of Consciousness

What does a literary technique have in common with sex therapy? You can use a stream-of-consciousness or free association technique to help yourself have erections.

Begin this session with focusing caresses. The man then lies on his back. The woman caresses the front of his body and his genitals in any way she enjoys. While the woman caresses, the man talks in a stream-of-consciousness style. This means that he says anything and everything that pops into his mind, without censoring anything.

There is no way to predict what you will talk about. Your "stream" may include random thoughts, grunts, moans, jokes, word lists, descriptions of how you feel, or descriptions of fantasies. Your female partner will not comment on anything you say.

The first time you do this exercise, you will be self-conscious and you will be lucky if you let out a minute's worth of unedited or uncensored material during a twenty-minute exercise.

This exercise is tough! It is probably the most difficult exercise that I have seen clients do. But it is worth it, because this exercise can help you get at unconscious material that may be interfering with your erection and arousal processes. In addition, talking while you are being stimulated interferes with the worrying and spectatoring that can slow down your erection process.

Sequence for Stream of Consciousness Exercise
Focusing caress — First person — 10 minutes
Focusing caress — Second person — 10 minutes
Stream of consciousness — 15 to 20 minutes
Feedback

Music Listening

The music listening exercise is similar to the stream of consciousness exercise. It is used for severe erection or inhibited ejaculation problems in men. It can help in cases of severe performance anxiety in partners of either sex, but is less used for this.

Most people can learn to focus on sensations of arousal in their genitals. But for some people, it is impossible to "turn off their head" and stop worrying about erection or orgasm. The solution is to provide some kind of stimulation that distracts the brain.

For this exercise, you will need a cassette player with headphones and a cassette of a type of music that you *don't* particularly like. A good tape to use would be something that provides a consistent low level of distraction and has little or no discernible musical quality, something that does not have lyrics, something that is mildly annoying. Don't use anything pleasant, such as a relaxation tape. A tape of white noise would work.

Begin with focusing caresses. The man then lies on his back listening to the tape while the woman stimulates his genitals in whatever way she enjoys. The tape will distract the man just enough so that he cannot worry about performance, but not enough to interfere with the erection or ejaculation reflexes.

Sequence for Music Listening
Focusing caress — First person — 10 minutes
Focusing caress — Second person — 10 minutes
Music listening — woman active — 15 to 30 minutes
Feedback

The exercises in this chapter may have helped you make a specific breakthrough, so that you can return to the main program. If after trying these breakthrough exercises you still feel that you are not making progress, it could be that your problem is more deep-rooted than you first thought. In that case you may need to explore other treatment options with a qualified therapist.

Chapter 16

❤

Developing Your Personal Program

This chapter contains guidelines on how to put together a series of exercises for yourself and your partner.

The exercises you will want to do will depend on whether one or both of you has a sexual problem, and the level of anxiety you each experience during sexual activity. Please note: All of the exercises described in this book are listed in Appendix II for easy reference.

Which Exercises Should We Do?

To begin, each partner should do the self-exercises, and these should be done alone. It will take about two weeks to complete the exercises you do by yourself. Begin to do exercises together after each partner has experience with self-caressing and peaking.

No matter what your area of interest or specific problem is, you and your partner should do all of the basic exercises together. These include spoon breathing, face caress, body image, back caress, front caress, genital caress, and oral genital caress. Doing these basic exercises will give you the foundation you need to begin to focus and relax, as well as help yourselves with your problem areas.

Make sure you are clear on the concepts that the basic exercises are meant to teach. If you did the exercises as suggested, you learned a number of important things. You learned to focus on sensations. You learned to relax and allow yourself to enjoy touch. You learned to touch for your own pleasure and not worry about your partner. You learned to stop thinking of sexual activity as a performance. You learned to give honest verbal feedback to your partner. If you feel comfortable with these concepts after doing the basic exercises, you are ready to move on.

Couples who are not experiencing problems will want to do those exercises that enhance their sensual enjoyment. I would recommend the basic exercises, and then the male peaking process and the exercises for female arousal.

❤

If one member of the couple has a specific sexual concern or problem, do the exercises described in the chapter for that problem. For example, if the man has a problem with premature ejaculation, the couple should do the peaking and plateauing exercises described in the chapter on premature ejaculation.

If one member of the couple has sexual anxiety or desire problems, or if the woman has vaginismus, the basic exercises should take care of the problem. You may then want to do some peaking or female arousal exercises to take yourselves from comfort to enjoyment.

If your sexual anxiety or vaginismus is fairly severe,

you may need to break the basic exercises into smaller parts. For example, instead of doing the back caress on the whole back of the body the first time, you may only be comfortable including the top half of the back. It is fine to break any of the exercises into smaller steps.

For this you can use the principle I mentioned earlier called "shaping," or "successive approximations of behavior." Psychologists use shaping to teach new behaviors to both humans and animals. Shaping means that you take small steps toward a goal, but you are always moving in the direction of the goal.

If the "goal" is to allow penetration of the vagina by the penis (as in vaginismus), the first step is to train the woman to relax her body. The first time her partner does a genital caress, she may become anxious if her partner keeps his hand on the vagina for more than a few seconds. The next time he does the genital caress, he may be able to keep his hand on the genitals for a minute or more. The next time, he may be able to move his hand on the genitals, and in the next session, the woman may be comfortable with finger penetration up to the first knuckle.

If sexual anxiety or vaginismus is the problem, you and your partner will be the best judges of how comfortable you are with each exercise. If you want to break an exercise into smaller, more comfortable parts, this is fine as long as both partners agree on the limits of the exercise beforehand. Just make sure that each step moves you conceptually closer and closer to your goal.

This same shaping principle applies to inhibited ejaculation. You may need to break the exercises into smaller steps, moving closer and closer to ejaculating in the vagina with each exercise.

❤

If both partners are having sexual difficulties, do the exercises for the man's problem first. The reason for this is that it will be easier for the woman to do the female arousal exercises successfully if her male partner can maintain an erection for some time. For example, if the man has a problem with rapid ejaculation and the woman has difficulty with orgasms, go through the peaking and plateauing process with the focus on the man. After he has had experience lasting longer, begin the peaking and plateauing process with the focus on the woman. Actually, the peaking process with the focus on the man is also quite enjoyable for the woman, who is often able to peak right along with the man because of the intensity of the sensate focus.

Although most of the exercises were designed for *specific* problems, they are also beneficial for other problems. For example, if a man has erection problems, he will want to do the exercises described in the chapter on erections. He then may want to go through the peaking process. Peaking is beneficial for erections because it puts the focus of attention on arousal rather than on erection, so it tends to decrease performance pressure.

You may need to repeat an exercise until you are comfortable with it. For example, a man may need to peak at low levels two or three times, or he may need to do the get-and-lose erection exercise a number of times.

Insert an exercise from the chapter on "Remembering to Play" once in a while to foster enjoyment. Use an exercise to reduce performance pressure if this continues to be a problem.

The way to get the most benefit from the exercises is to do them in order, because they build on each other. For example, I would not do a peaking exercise together until I had done all of the basic exercises in order. You need experience with repeating the sensate focus process before you will receive the maximum enjoyment and benefit from later exercises.

How Often Should We Do Exercises?

One to three exercises a week will be optimal. One exercise a day is too much, as you and your partner need some time to internalize the changes that will take place in your bodies and your minds. However, if you do an exercise together less than once a week, you probably will not retain the gains you have made.

Use the charts at the end of this chapter to plan a program for yourself. Keep in mind that you and your partner will have the best chance of enriching your mutual sexuality and helping your problems if you set a schedule at the beginning of each week and try to stick to it. Remember that you don't need to be in a sexy mood to do an exercise—you only have to want to do the exercise.

Also remember that while the exercises contain an "ideal" structure of what should happen, there are no demands on you to have an erection, have an orgasm, or control an ejaculation in any exercise. Enjoy whatever happens and learn about your body and its natural response.

When you schedule your exercises for the week, be sure to set aside enough time and make sure that you will have the use of a room in which you won't be disturbed. This is *essential* for your ability to relax.

If you and your partner have trouble agreeing on when to do the exercises or how often to do them, it may help to use a contract. You may need to write down what you agree to do and sign this agreement. This is a very common practice in many types of therapy and may give you a motivational boost.

How Long Will This Program Take?

Try not to rush through the program. Remember that the slower you go, the more you will enjoy yourself and the more lasting the gains will be. If you have a doubt about whether to repeat an exercise or move ahead, repeat the exercise, as this will lock in the gains you have made.

You will see a change in yourself and the way you respond after the basic exercises, but you may not see changes from exercise to exercise. It is best to give yourself time to do three or four exercises before you ask yourself, "How am I responding differently?" Remember that you have the best chance of helping yourself if you go into this program with the attitude that you will enjoy yourself, rather than worrying about making progress.

If you or your partner has a sexual problem, be aware that there is no "quick fix." Chances are that you have had the problem for some time, and it is going to take some amount of time for your attitudes and behaviors to change. One exercise will not be a miracle cure. You need to learn a new way to be sensual and sexual, and this requires *practice*.

If you do exercises together twice a week, the average sexual problem will take about two to six months to treat. Inhibited ejaculation can take as long as twelve months. You will be able to see results at various points in the program.

If you find that your problem is so severe that you do not respond to these exercises, you may need to seek help from a qualified sex therapist. This does not mean that you have failed. Some people are more able to learn things from books, while others learn better from people. A urologist, psychologist, marriage counselor, or social worker should be able to refer you to a sex therapist.

How will you know whether the sex therapist you are referred to is capable? A good sex therapist who specializes in the psychological treatment of sexual problems should describe a treatment program that is very similar to the one described in this book. This means that the therapist will have you and your partner do activities together, rather than just talk to you. A good sex therapist will also rule out any physical causes for your problems before proceeding with treatment. If you are single and need to work with a surrogate partner, you need to make this clear to your therapist. Surrogate partners are available in major metropolitan areas.

TYPICAL THERAPY PROGRAMS

In this section I will list typical progressions of exercises that clients have used to treat their sexual problems. Keep in mind that these are not set in stone, and once you have completed the self-exercises and the basic exercises with your partner, you may need to break future exercises into smaller steps or repeat some exercises.

Sexual Anxiety,
Sexual Desire Problems, Sexual Healing.

The essential sets of exercises are the self-exercises, the basic sensate focus exercises, and the peaking process for both men and women. These are the most important facets of the program for people who have no functional problems, but would like to experience greater intimacy and more arousal in their relationship (we'll call this a sexual healing program). They are also the basis for dealing with any sexual problem.

Self Exercises
Breathing
PC Muscle exercises
Pelvic Thrusts and Rolls
Body Self-caress
Genital Self-caress
Arousal Awareness
Peaking — low levels
Peaking — high levels
Plateauing

Basic Exercises With Your Partner
Spoon Breathing
Face Caress
Body Image
Back Caress
Front Caress
Genital Caress
Oral Sex

Advanced Exercises With Your Partner
Male Arousal Monitoring — manual or oral
Male Peaking — manual or oral — low levels
Male Peaking — manual or oral — high levels
Nondemand Penetration
Male Vaginal Peaking — woman active
Male Vaginal Peaking — man active
Male Plateauing
Female Arousal Monitoring
Female Peaking — manual or oral — low levels
Female Peaking — manual or oral — high levels
Female Vaginal Peaking — man active
Female Vaginal Peaking — woman active
Female Plateauing

Optional
Genital Caress with Verbal Feedback
Foot Caress
Sensuous Shower
Tom Jones Dinner
Sensuous Kissing
Towel Over the Face
Ask For What You Want
Zombie
Switch Focus
Mutual Masturbation
Sensate Focus Intercourse

❤

If you have no specific sexual dysfunction and you would like to use the sensate focus exercises to enhance your sex life, you could experience the male peaking process first and then begin the female peaking process. Or, to foster intimacy in your relationship, you could alternate the male and female peaking exercises, so that each partner is able to learn about the other's response to the same exercise.

Premature Ejaculation

This is a typical progression of exercises for dealing with rapid ejaculation. After the man feels his ejaculation is under control, you may wish to experience female arousal training also.

The man who is trying to learn to control his ejaculations will need to repeat the PC muscle exercises, self-peaking, and self-plateauing throughout the entire program. If you have had difficulty controlling your ejaculation at any time in your life, you should probably continue the self-peaking exercises twice a week for the rest of your life, especially if you have no steady sexual partner.

The peaking process is the most important series of exercises for premature ejaculation. If you have a severe premature ejaculation problem, you may need to repeat each peaking exercise a number of times.

Self Exercises
Breathing
PC Muscle exercises
Pelvic Thrusts and Rolls
Body Self-caress
Genital Self-caress
Arousal Awareness

Peaking — low levels
Peaking — high levels
Plateauing

Basic Exercises With Your Partner
Spoon Breathing
Face Caress
Body Image
Back Caress
Front Caress
Genital Caress
Oral Sex

Advanced Exercises With Your Partner
Genital Caress with Verbal Feedback
Male Arousal Monitoring
Male Peaking — manual or oral — low levels
Male Peaking — manual or oral — high levels
Male Peaking — manual or oral — man active
Nondemand Penetration
Male Vaginal Peaking — woman active
Male Vaginal Peaking — man active
Male Vaginal Plateauing

Optional
Keeping Physical and Emotional Charge Together
PC Squeeze
Squeeze Technique
Foot Caress
Sensuous Shower
Tom Jones Dinner
Sensuous Kissing
Towel Over the Face
Ask For What You Want
Zombie
Switch Focus

Mutual Masturbation
Sensate Focus Intercourse
Female Arousal Monitoring
Female Peaking — manual or oral — low levels
Female Peaking — manual or oral — high levels
Female Vaginal Peaking — man active
Female Vaginal Peaking — woman active
Female Plateauing

Vaginismus

This is a typical progression of exercises for dealing with vaginismus. Depending on the level of your anxiety, you may need to break the basic exercises (especially the genital caress) into a series of smaller steps with which you are more comfortable.

Self Exercises
Breathing
PC Muscle exercises
Pelvic Thrusts and Rolls
Body Self-caress
Genital Self-caress
Arousal Awareness
Peaking — low levels
Peaking — high levels
Plateauing

Basic Exercises With Your Partner
Spoon Breathing
Face Caress
Body Image
Back Caress
Front Caress
Genital Caress
Oral Sex

Advanced Exercises With Your Partner
Genital Caress with Verbal Feedback
Female Arousal Monitoring
Female Peaking — manual or oral — low levels
Female Peaking — manual or oral — high levels
Female Vaginal Peaking — man active
Female Vaginal Peaking — woman active
Female Plateauing

Optional
Male Arousal Monitoring — manual or oral
Male Peaking — manual or oral — low levels
Male Peaking — manual or oral — high levels
Nondemand Penetration
Male Vaginal Peaking — woman active
Male Vaginal Peaking — man active
Male Plateauing
Foot Caress
Sensuous Shower
Tom Jones Dinner
Sensuous Kissing
Towel Over the Face
Ask For What You Want
Zombie
Switch Focus
Mutual Masturbation
Sensate Focus Intercourse

Female Arousal and Orgasm Problems

Here is a typical progression of exercises for a woman who has trouble becoming aroused or reaching orgasm. In order to maximize the woman's ability to become aroused, the couple may wish to have the man experience the peaking process first, even if he has had no problem.

Self Exercises
Breathing
PC Muscle exercises
Pelvic Thrusts and Rolls
Body Self-caress
Genital Self-caress
Arousal Awareness
Peaking — low levels
Peaking — high levels
Plateauing

Basic Exercises With Your Partner
Spoon Breathing
Face Caress
Body Image
Back Caress
Front Caress
Genital Caress
Oral Sex

Advanced Exercises With Your Partner
Genital Caress With Verbal Feedback
Female Arousal Monitoring
Female Peaking — manual or oral — low levels
Female Peaking — manual or oral — high levels
Female Vaginal Peaking — man active
Female Vaginal Peaking — woman active
Female Plateauing

Optional
Male Arousal Monitoring — manual or oral
Male Peaking — manual or oral — low levels
Male Peaking — manual or oral — high levels
Nondemand Penetration
Male Vaginal Peaking — woman active
Male Vaginal Peaking — man active

Male Plateauing
Foot Caress
Sensuous Shower
Tom Jones Dinner
Sensuous Kissing
Towel Over the Face
Ask For What You Want
Zombie
Switch Focus
Mutual Masturbation
Sensate Focus Intercourse
Faking Orgasm

Erection Problems

This is a typical progression of exercises for a man with erection problems. You may both wish to go through the peaking process before you start to deal with the erection problems.

Self Exercises
Breathing
PC Muscle exercises
Pelvic Thrusts and Rolls
Body Self-caress
Genital Self-caress
Arousal Awareness
Peaking — low levels
Peaking — high levels
Plateauing

Basic Exercises With Your Partner
Spoon Breathing
Face Caress
Body Image
Back Caress
Front Caress

Genital Caress
Oral Sex

Advanced Exercises With Your Partner
Genital Caress with Verbal Feedback
Flaccid Insertion
Erection Awareness
Get and Lose Erections
Maintaining Erections During Intercourse

Optional
Male Arousal Monitoring — manual or oral
Male Peaking — manual or oral — low levels
Male Peaking — manual or oral — high levels
Nondemand Penetration
Male Vaginal Peaking — woman active
Male Vaginal Peaking — man active
Male Plateauing
Female Arousal Monitoring
Female Peaking — manual or oral — low levels
Female Peaking — manual or oral — high levels
Female Vaginal Peaking — man active
Female Vaginal Peaking — woman active
Female Plateauing
Foot Caress
Sensuous Shower
Tom Jones Dinner
Sensuous Kissing
Towel Over the Face
Ask For What You Want
Zombie
Switch Focus
Mutual Masturbation
Sensate Focus Intercourse
Stream of Consciousness
Music Listening

If you have had erection problems in the past, you should continue the self-peaking process throughout the remainder of the program. You should make sure that you keep the circulation system in your penis in shape by creating a daily erection by yourself.

Inhibited Ejaculation

Here are two typical progressions of exercises for dealing with inhibited ejaculation. Try the simpler one that involves the peaking process first. If you still have difficulty ejaculating in the vagina, move on to the second series.

Progression #1

Self Exercises
Breathing
PC Muscle exercises
Pelvic Thrusts and Rolls
Body Self-caress
Genital Self-caress
Arousal Awareness
Peaking — low levels
Peaking — high levels
Plateauing

Basic Exercises With Your Partner
Spoon Breathing
Face Caress
Body Image
Back Caress
Front Caress
Genital Caress
Oral Sex

Advanced Exercises With Your Partner
Genital Caress with Verbal Feedback
Male Arousal Monitoring
Male Peaking — manual or oral — low levels
Male Peaking — manual or oral — high levels
Male Peaking — manual or oral — man active
Nondemand Penetration
Male Vaginal Peaking — woman active
Male Vaginal Peaking — man active
Male Vaginal Plateauing
Intercourse with Masturbation

Progression #2

Self Exercises
Breathing
PC Muscle exercises
Pelvic Thrusts and Rolls
Body Self-caress
Genital Self-caress
Arousal Awareness
Peaking — low levels
Peaking — high levels
Plateauing

Basic Exercises With Your Partner
Spoon Breathing
Face Caress
Body Image
Back Caress
Front Caress
Genital Caress
Oral Sex

Advanced Exercises With Your Partner
Genital Caress with Verbal Feedback
Male Arousal Monitoring

Male Peaking — manual or oral — low levels
Male Peaking — manual or oral — high levels
Male Peaking — manual or oral — man active
Nondemand Penetration
Male Vaginal Peaking — woman active
Male Vaginal Peaking — man active
Male Vaginal Plateauing
Intercourse with Masturbation
Alternating Intercourse with Masturbation
Masturbate to ejaculation
with your partner in the room
Masturbate to ejaculation
with your partner on the bed next to you watching
Masturbate to ejaculation
and ejaculate on your partner's stomach
Masturbate to ejaculation
and ejaculate at the entrance to your partner's vagina
Masturbate to ejaculation
while on your back and signal your partner
to climb on top as you are ejaculating
Masturbate to ejaculation
while kneeling in front of your partner
and thrust into the vagina as you ejaculate
Masturbate, peak, and penetrate at level "9." Ejaculate
in the vagina with your hand on your penis
Masturbate during intercourse and remove your hand
as you ejaculate

Optional
Female Arousal Monitoring
Female Peaking — manual or oral — low levels
Female Peaking — manual or oral — high levels
Female Vaginal Peaking — man active
Female Vaginal Peaking — woman active
Female Plateauing
Foot Caress

Sensuous Shower
Tom Jones Dinner
Sensuous Kissing
Towel Over the Face
Ask For What You Want
Zombie
Switch Focus
Mutual Masturbation
Sensate Focus Intercourse
Stream of Consciousness
Music Listening

If you have a severe problem with inhibited ejaculation, you may need to repeat each step in this process a number of times. You should also continue the self-peaking process throughout the program.

❤

Sexual Healing is unique in that it gives you specific, detailed ways of enhancing your sexuality and dealing with common problems. The programs I have outlined above have worked again and again for hundreds of clients. After you have done the exercises once, don't hesitate to improvise on them, or make up your own using the basic sensate focus principles.

Chapter 17

❤

Sexual Healing: Beyond Sensate Focus

The exercises in *Sexual Healing* have taught you to relax and focus on your sensual and sexual feelings. Your sexual experiences are richer now, and if you were experiencing a sexual problem, it is probably a thing of the past. In addition, when you and your partner experienced the exercises, you probably had moments during which your shared focus resulted in increased feelings of intimacy. You can now use your newfound ability to become sexually aroused to heal your mind, your body, and your relationship with your partner.

Healing Your Mind

We have already seen in the chapter on "Sexuality: Body and Mind" that physical activity can be beneficial to your mental health—it can help to alleviate anxiety and depression. Your ability to relax and concentrate on one thing at a time will carry over into other aspects of your life.

The sexual activities you have learned in *Sexual Healing* can also promote confidence and self-esteem. You feel better about yourself not only because you have learned to enjoy sexual expression, but also because you know that your partner enjoys what you do and is able to become sexually aroused with you.

How can I make these claims? When I work with clients, I often see people who are extremely anxious and depressed, not only because of their sexual problems but also because of their lack of satisfying social relationships.

One client in particular stands out in my mind. I'll call him Gary. The first time I met Gary, he entered the room hunched over and could not look me in the eye. He stammered when he talked and looked as if he wanted to run away. He was one of the most anxious and withdrawn people I had ever met.

It was extremely gratifying for me to see that after only a few sessions of therapy, he walked into the room with perfect posture, exuding self-confidence. He looked his therapist and me in the eye and talked animatedly. (He had even bought new clothes!) I hope that interacting with your partner in a nondemand way and learning to communicate honestly about your sexual experiences have begun to have the same effect on you.

In addition to reducing anxiety and depression and building your self-esteem and confidence, the sexual healing exercises can also heal your mind by providing you with positive memories to look back on, instead of the "negative tapes" with which you may have started the program. The sensate focus technique, because it is a concentration technique, improves your ability to remember the positive sexual experiences you have had.

Healing Your Body

In the chapter "Sexuality: Body and Mind," I outlined some of the ways in which breathing, touch, and deep muscle relaxation can have a positive effect on your health. As we have seen, there is a long tradition in psychology linking mental and physical health.

Anxiety is a health-destroyer. In the sexual healing program, you learned to recognize anxiety and deal with it. You also learned to slow your body down and promote the action of your parasympathetic (relaxation) nervous system, which can also benefit your health.

Stress is another health-destroyer. The relaxing sexual activity that you have learned to experience with your partner can provide an antidote to the body tension that has built up from stress over the day or week.

Perhaps most important, sexual expression can provide a "natural high." Sexual activity beginning from a relaxed state allows your brain to produce endorphins, our natural painkillers. Instead of numbing yourself with alcohol or drugs and getting sex "over with," you can now use relaxing sexual activity to promote your physical health.

To my knowledge, no psychologist has studied exactly what kind of sexual activity releases endorphins. But I know from experience that the *peaking process* seems to train your brain to systematically release these chemicals. Exercises that involve mutual peaking at high levels of arousal seem to be best for simply making you feel good, physically and mentally.

Healing Your Relationship

You and your partner learned many things in the sexual healing program that can benefit your relationship. You learned to shut out the world temporarily and concentrate totally on each other. You learned to set aside time for each other and to communicate honestly about your sexual feelings in a nonthreatening way. You learned to have "clean" interactions with each other in the here and now, rather than dwell on past unpleasantness.

There is a state beyond what you have experienced so far in the sexual healing program. That state is mutuality—a feeling that you and your partner are really *together*. Many of the exercises in this program required you to take turns with the active and passive roles. You and your partner can begin to promote mutuality by doing different activities at the same time. You have enough experience with focusing that you can switch your focus to your partner and back to yourself again without worrying about performance or becoming anxious.

Paradoxically, another way to promote mutuality or intimacy is by taking turns making love to each other. Before you had the experience of learning to focus on your own feelings, it would have been difficult for you to do this and feel confident about it. But now you have done nondemand activities with each other in which you watched your partner become aroused, possibly all the way to orgasm. You now know not only how your partner becomes aroused, but also how to take pleasure for yourself while enjoying your partner's response.

Have your partner lie back and relax. Pleasure yourself using your partner's body. Keep your eyes locked on your partner's eyes as you psychologically draw your partner in and compel your partner to focus on what you are doing by focusing intensely yourself. What will draw your partner in is the intensity of your focus plus your partner's certainty that you are doing what *you* enjoy.

What the sexual healing program has given you is *options*. You now have the choice of having a "quickie" if you want to, or having a long, slow, focused, intimate episode of intercourse. You have the option of using sexual activity as a source of mental or physical healing or using it to express lust or animal desire. You can have sexual intercourse in order to feel closeness with your partner or to simply feel good about moving your body and "getting off." You have the option of multiple orgasms or no orgasms at all if you wish.

After you have completed the exercises in this book, *go back and do some of the basics again,* such as the face caress. Your experience with the sexual healing exercises has changed you by making you more aware of your responses and your partner's responses. This experience has changed your way of looking at the world. Now, if you go back and redo a face caress or another exercise you did early in the program, you will look for and get something completely different from it.

Is Ecstasy in Your Future?

In the sexual healing program, you have made the transition from discomfort with or limitation in sexual activities to comfort, enjoyment, and arousal. My goal in writing *Sexual Healing* has been to present *practical* information that you can use to attain comfort and arousal. In other words, I have tried to describe the sexual and sensual exercises in this program on a rather basic body and feeling level.

As you and your partner may have already discovered while doing the sensate focus exercises, there is a level of sexual experience beyond arousal, and even beyond mutuality or intimacy. This is "ecstasy." It is the feeling that you and your partner are so close during a sexual encounter that you temporarily transcend the physical, material plane and have a highly intimate, or spiritual, experience as you have intercourse and orgasm together.

The exercises in *Sexual Healing* can provide you with the sensual mindset necessary to understand and experience ecstasy. Spiritual experiences are always highly personal, so I cannot describe a "typical" ecstatic moment. Some people have said they see intense colors or images; others hear music; some feel an overwhelming sense of connection with all of creation.

The ecstasy associated with intense sexual experiences is the focus of a form of yoga, known as tantra. After you have completed the exercises in *Sexual Healing*, you may wish to learn more about tantric yoga or tantric sex in order to go further in your exploration of your sexual self.

❤

We live in an era in which much of the information presented publicly about sex is negative. A focus on the harmful aspects of sexuality (such as the transmission of diseases) may cause us to overlook the overwhelmingly positive effects sexual expression can have on our lives. I hope that the sensual activities you have learned here will help you to enjoy the many soothing and healthy aspects of sexuality—increased sexual self-esteem, feelings of personal fulfillment, intimacy with a partner, and sexual ecstasy.

Appendix I

❤

The Sensual Mindset
& Guidelines for Feedback

The list below, which is a repeat of the summary at the end of Chapter 5, contains the basic instructions for approaching and doing *any* sensate focus exercise.

I call these instructions "The Sensual Mindset" because, taken together, they represent an attitude toward sensual sexual experience. As long as you follow these guidelines when doing the exercises in this book, you will derive all the benefit the exercises are designed to deliver, *no matter what the "apparent" results are.* Remember, the most important goal of this program is to expand your personal sensual awareness. The sensual mindset will enhance all your sexual experiences, possibly in ways that you and I could never predict.

I suggest you come back to this list again and again until the ideas in it become second nature to you.

The Sensual Mindset

1. Always focus on the point of contact where your skin touches your partner's skin.

2. When you are active, do the exercise for your own pleasure and do not worry whether your partner is enjoying it. Use a slow, light caressing technique.

3. Stay passive when in the passive role.

4. Stay in the here and now.

5. Focus on sensual pleasure rather than sexual arousal.

6. If anxiety does not quickly decrease after the first few minutes of an exercise, ask your partner to go back to a less advanced exercise.

7. Don't work at it.

8. Agree on the limits of the exercise beforehand and do not go beyond those limits.

9. Provide honest feedback after the exercise.

To sum up still more concisely: Focus on the touch, breathe evenly, and relax your muscles.

Focus, breathe, relax.

❤

Guidelines for Feedback

After each exercise, you and your partner will give feedback to each other about how you felt during the exercise. Use the following questions as guidelines for what to talk about.

1. When you were passive, were you able to relax and accept pleasure for yourself? Did you feel pressured to do something to convince your partner that he or she was doing a good job? Did you enjoy the caress? Did the touch feel like a caress or like a massage? Was it mechanical?

    If your touch is perceived by your partner as being rough, fast, or mechanical, you may need to adjust your caressing technique.

2. During the active role, did you take pleasure for yourself rather than worry about whether your partner was enjoying the caress? Did you feel pressured to perform, or did you touch your partner the way you wanted to touch? Did you enjoy the caress? How much of the time did you do the exercise for your own pleasure? Did you wonder what your partner was thinking about?

    When you are active, you should be able to take pleasure for yourself most of the time. If you really focus during the active role, thoughts about your partner should not enter your mind. The exception would be if you can see by outward physical signs that the passive partner is not relaxing.

3. Which role were you more comfortable with, the active or the passive role? Was it easier for you to focus in one role than in the other? Which role was more enjoyable for you, active or passive? Why?

4. What part of the time were you able to focus on the touch when you were active? When you were passive? If you had a problem staying focused, what type of thoughts distracted you?

    Ideally, you should be focusing on the touch most of the time. If you are not able to focus this much, repeat the exercise as many times as you need to until you are able to do so. It may be helpful to examine the types of thoughts that are interfering with your concentration. If mundane things intrude, such as the laundry or the shopping list, you probably just haven't had enough practice in focusing—it may take a few more sessions. If you are having thoughts or anxieties about future exercises, this is normal—tell yourself you can worry about these things at some other time, so they don't interfere with your practice.

5. Did you feel anxious during the caress? Were you able to deal with that anxiety by focusing, breathing, and relaxing? Could you feel yourself becoming less anxious as the caress went on?

   The important thing is not how high or low your anxiety level was at any point during the caress; the important thing is that you are less anxious after the caress than before. After each exercise, each partner should report on his or her anxiety level during the exercise, and his or her perception of the partner's anxiety level. You may want to use a scale of 1–10 to help you talk about the anxiety, with "1" being no anxiety and "10" being extreme anxiety.

6. Did either partner experience sexual arousal during the exercise? If you felt aroused, did you just accept it and keep your attention on where you were being touched, or did you try to make the arousal better, or get rid of it?

   It may make it easier to talk about arousal levels if you use a numerical scale, as you learned in the self-caressing exercises and as you have done for anxiety levels, above.

7. Did each person stay within the bounds of the exercise, or did one or both partners attempt to go beyond the limits?

   It is natural to want to continue and do something more sexual, but in order to build trust it is important to do what you both agree to do in the beginning.

8. Did each person feel the exercise was in general a positive experience?

❤

Did you have a problem with feeling anxious? If so, you need to focus on your breathing. Did you have a problem remaining passive? If so, you need to relax your stomach, thigh, and buttocks muscles. Did you have a problem staying in the here and now? Did you want to please your partner? Were you working at doing a good job? You need to practice focusing on the touch. Did you have a problem focusing? You may need to caress more slowly. Most of the problems you encounter can be resolved in three words: *focus, breathe, relax.*

Appendix II

❤

A List of
Sensate Focus Exercises

Exercises to Do by Yourself
Breathing 62
PC Muscle exercises 63
Pelvic Thrusts and Rolls 67
Body Self-caress 68
Genital Self-caress 69
Arousal Awareness 71
Peaking — low levels 72
Peaking — high levels 73
Plateauing 75

Basic Sensate Focus Exercises
Spoon Breathing 95
Face Caress 96
Body Image 103
Back Caress 110

Front Caress 119
Genital Caress 125
Genital Caress with Feedback 129
Oral Genital Caress 130

Remembering to Play
Foot Caress 136
Sensuous Shower 138
Tom Jones Dinner 138
Finding the G Spot 140
Sexological Exam 140

Exercises for Rapid Ejaculation
Male Arousal Monitoring 143
Male Peaking — manual or oral — low levels 150
Male Peaking — manual or oral — high levels 151
Male Peaking — manual or oral — man active 153
Nondemand Penetration 154
Male Vaginal Peaking — woman active 157
Male Vaginal Peaking — man active 159
Male Peaking — man active and on top 160
Male Plateauing 163
Keeping Physical and Emotional Charge Together 164

Exercises for Erection Problems
Flaccid Insertion 168
Erection Awareness 170
Getting and Losing Erections 172
Maintaining Erections During Intercourse 176

Exercises for Female Arousal
Female Arousal Monitoring 182
Female Peaking — manual or oral — man active 184
Female Vaginal Peaking — man active 186
Female Vaginal Peaking — woman active 188
Female Plateauing — manual or oral 191

Appendix III

———— ❤ ————

My Work
as a Surrogate Partner

I am often asked to give guest lectures about surrogate work to university classes in human sexuality and counseling. I find that the majority of students in these classes do not know what surrogate partners are or what we do. I usually give a brief presentation on sexual problems and then allow the students to ask questions or provide comments and opinions. (There are always comments and opinions!) I have prepared this chapter based on the questions that are usually asked of me during these presentations. I hope that this information will help dispel any confusion or mystique surrounding surrogate partners as well as give you a better understanding about what we do.

What is a surrogate partner?

You will notice that I refer to myself as a surrogate

partner rather than as a "sex surrogate" (a phrase with which you may be more familiar). We have adopted the term "surrogate partner" to reflect the fact that we do much more than have sexual intercourse with clients. In fact, sexual intercourse makes up only a small part of what we do. The majority of our work concerns sensuality, not sexuality.

In general, surrogate partners work with clients in behavioral exercises similar to those you have read in this book. In addition to working directly on sexual problems, surrogates coach clients in social skills, such as asking for dates.

Surrogate partners work only under the supervision of a licensed therapist. Surrogate partner therapy is an adjunct to therapy and surrogate partners are hired by the therapist, not by the clients. If you have heard of a surrogate partner working with a client without a therapist, be aware that this is unethical and is not the norm for professional surrogate partners.

Do not confuse surrogate *partners* with surrogate *mothers*. Surrogate partners are trained persons who work with clients who are experiencing sexual problems; surrogate mothers bear children for women who are unable to have their own (this is not a sexual dysfunction).

Why are surrogate partners used?

In sex therapy, the ideal situation is for two partners who are committed to each other to work together on the problem. Sometimes this is not possible. In the case of single persons who are experiencing severe sexual problems, their very problem may prevent them from seeking out partners, although that is the thing that could help them the most. These people are in an extremely unhappy state, especially if the sexual problem has been a part of their life for some time and if they have already tried a type of therapy that did not work. A surrogate partner can be the answer.

Surrogate partners have been found to be extremely effective in teaching clients new sexual behaviors. Learning by watching someone else do the desired behavior, called "modeling" or "observational learning" by psychologists, is known to be a very powerful method of learning. Learning by observing has often proved to be more effective than learning by reading or having someone tell you about something, which is the way many sex therapists currently attempt to change their clients' sexual behaviors.

Many clients need someone to show them how to touch, how to be sensual, and how to engage in various sexual practices. It is unethical for therapists to physically touch their clients, even if their intentions are positive and worthwhile. So the therapist may call in a surrogate partner to be the person to actually work skin-to-skin with the client.

Clients may find it easier to open up to a person who is more like a peer and less like an authority figure. It is quite common for clients to provide the surrogate partner with personal information that they would feel uncomfortable telling the therapist. The intimate context of sharing sexual activities can lead people to disclose highly personal information. So we say that surrogate partner therapy provides "grist for the therapist's mill"— working with the surrogate partner brings up important information that the therapist would have been unable to find out alone.

Here is an example of what I am talking about. A male surrogate partner I know began to work with a female client who had been in long-term psychotherapy with a psychiatrist. Her stated problem was that she was unable to enjoy sex or reach orgasm. During her very first surrogate session, which was a nonsexual exercise, she volunteered that she had had an incestuous relationship—a fact that she had never mentioned in her years of psychotherapy.

I also have had clients tell me things of this nature. They may not intentionally withhold this information from their therapist; rather, something in the surrogate session may stir a memory or finally make them sufficiently comfortable to talk of it.

Surrogate partners can be valuable when, as often happens, clients don't have the sexual experience, knowledge, or vocabulary to describe the nature and extent of their problem. For example, we often hear clients say that they are impotent, when in fact the problem is that they ejaculate quickly. People use the term "impotence" to refer to virtually any type of male sexual problem, a confusion that itself can cause problems!

If a therapist attempted to treat clients like this with talk therapy, the treatment, based on a misunderstanding, would be unlikely to succeed. Surrogate partners have the training and experience to accurately assess what the client's sexual problem is. For example, I had a client who said he was having erection problems. When I began to do sensual exercises with him, I found rather that he ejaculated during the most basic exercises. The chances are, working only with words, the therapist would not have found out what the client's real problem was until much later, if at all.

Occasionally we have clients report that they are functional, but that they seem to turn their partners off and they don't know why. A surrogate partner can determine exactly what the client is doing. For example, clients may unknowingly put too much psychological pressure on their partners or use nonverbal cues that are irritating or distracting.

Jim was such a client. He had been with many women sexually but was beginning to have problems with erections because women would go to bed with him a few times and then not want to see him again.

What he was doing soon became apparent. Although he could get erections, during sexual intercourse he simply looked so uninterested that it was no wonder that women did not want to continue a relationship. To look at his face, you would think that he was bored or even irritated. This facial expression did not reflect his true feelings—he actually enjoyed sex but was a rather shy and inhibited person.

Besides doing exercises to increase his sexual responsiveness and sensuality, we also practiced expressing emotions and verbally communicating feelings of sexual pleasure. Learning to express his emotions probably helped him more in establishing relationships than did clearing up his difficulties with erection, but if he had not worked with a surrogate partner chances are that his therapist would not have found out about his problem.

If surrogate partner therapy has so many benefits, why don't more therapists use surrogate partners with their clients?

Therapists and clients are often unaware that surrogate partners are available. In addition, most of what is presented in the media about surrogate partners is negative. For example, talk shows on which surrogate partners are interviewed often include some fairly harsh audience commentary.

Some sex therapists who are willing to use surrogate partners don't understand what the partners are for. I once worked for a therapist who told her client—while I was present—that the main reason I was there was to fill all of his sexual needs, and she didn't understand why I objected to this.

Finally, many well-known sex therapists have been using surrogate partners with their clients for years and not publicly admitting it. The secrecy surrounding the use of surrogate partners has perhaps conveyed the impression that they are not often used.

What are the types of people with whom surrogate partners work?

The most common type of client is one who has a sexual dysfunction, such as difficulties with erection, premature ejaculation, or inability to reach orgasm. We also see persons who are afraid of sexual activity, or have remained virgin until a relatively late age (thirty or older). I have had handicapped clients and clients with other physical problems that make it difficult for them to seek out partners. They may be curious about what they are able to do sexually or would like to learn to express themselves sexually. Some clients are sexually functional but lack social skills. In such cases, the emphasis is on helping the client learn to be more comfortable in social and intimate personal situations.

The majority of our clients are single persons. Some are separated or going through a divorce. Occasionally, with his or her spouse's consent, a married person will work with a surrogate partner.

Some clients have sexual problems other than actual dysfunction. Surrogate partners, especially male partners, work with clients who have been sexually traumatized in some way, such as victims of rape or incest. Surrogate partners have worked with child molesters, providing an example of a more appropriate peer-level sexual relationship. Surrogate partners are sometimes called in to work with fetishists, exhibitionists, transvestites, or other people with sexual variations—not necessarily to change the person's orientation but rather to show the person so-called normal sexuality by way of comparison.

Besides doing the specific exercises that you read about, surrogate partners provide an accepting atmosphere in which the client can explore his or her sexuality without fear of rejection or ridicule. Sometimes the surrogate partner is providing the first intimate relationship that the client has ever had, and often the surrogate partner is providing the first relationship in which both partners communicate honestly and openly.

The clients who have the best chance of benefiting from surrogate partner therapy are those with sexual dysfunction but no psychiatric problems, who are motivated to change. Surrogate partner therapy (like other psychological therapy) generally works well for clients who are of average or above average intelligence, although surrogate partners could certainly be used to teach the mentally handicapped appropriate sexual behaviors.

What is the difference between a surrogate partner and a prostitute?

There are obvious similarities, but the social roles and expectations are very different. The surrogate situation is supervised by a licensed psychologist or counselor, who designs a complete program of treatment. The context is one of trained professional therapy. The goal of immediate sexual gratification is secondary, or this goal may not exist at all. The major goals are instead education and training in sensuality so that the client learns what he or she can do sexually and what he or she likes to do. The majority of surrogate partner therapy sessions do not include intercourse and many sessions do not include genital stimulation.

surrogate partners work with female clients who have been so sexually traumatized by a man that they cannot bear to be touched by any man. Gay surrogate partners have also been available to work with male or female gay clients.

What is the professional status of surrogate partners?

Surrogate partners have no formalized professional status. They are privately trained and there is no government licensing. Thus, there is currently no way for prospective clients to judge whether surrogate partners meet any established standard of training or experience. Surrogate partners do have a professional association—IPSA (International Professional Surrogate Association)—which has drawn up a code of ethics including the rule of working only under the guidance of trained and licensed therapists.

How has AIDS affected surrogate work?

The sexual exercises that I do with clients and which you will learn in this book are consistent with the practice of safe sex. Since most of the sensual exercises do not involve the exchange of body fluids, AIDS is not an issue for the initial part of the program. Prior to any sexual exercises, I require that all potential clients be tested for HIV antibodies as well as venereal diseases. In addition, most surrogate partners now require the use of condoms and nonoxynol-9 spermicide for sexual intercourse.

Any objections clients raise to the use of condoms are issues that themselves require discussion. The reality of life in the 1990s is such that when a client's sexual problems have been resolved and he or she attempts to start relationships out in the real world, many potential partners will require the use of condoms.

In fact, a surrogate partner is unlikely to contract AIDS from a client, because most clients are not able to function sexually. I have never heard of a surrogate partner contracting a venereal disease from a client. For that matter, I have never heard of a surrogate partner having a sexually transmitted disease.

To sum up: Surrogate partners are not people with mysterious sexual abilities or knowledge. We are people who have learned how to deal with sexual problems, how to enjoy sexuality, and how to avoid sexual pressure—all of the things you have learned in *Sexual Healing*.

———————————— ❤ ————————————

If you would like more information about surrogate partners or have a question about any specific issue discussed in the book, please write to the author at the following address:

Dr. Barbara Keesling
c/o Hunter House Inc., Publishers
P.O. Box 847
Claremont CA 91711, U.S.A.